Christmastime
Between the Vines

by Jamie Mills-Price

From the Author

After many requests over the years, (see we do listen!) I have been able to finally complete a book devoted entirely to Christmas. I hope you enjoy painting from it as much as I did in preparing it for you. If you have the time let me know if you liked this idea or not. You can e-mail me at my address below. I do get alot of e-mail, so please be patient with me if you are waiting for a reply! My website has been down for a while now, but should be up and running by the time this book is released. If you have any questions and/or would like info on my Summer Seminar (held locally) e-mail me at info@between-thevines.com. For a brochure of my pattern packets, technique sheets or books please send $1.00 to the address below. Happy Painting!

Dedication

I would like to dedicate this book to my two wonderful sons, Ryan and Tyler. Thank you from the bottom of my heart...for being the most responsible, respectful, loving children that a Mom could ask for. (smile) I am truly blessed and so very proud of you both. I love you!

Special Thanks

Appreciation goes out (again) to all the wonderful woodmen/craftsmen who supply me with great surfaces to paint on. Thanks!!

A special thank you to that big, loveable & huggable bear - Don @ Valhalla Designs...he has taken over the business from Ceal and Jim and is new to this industry ... give him a hard time at the conventions for me, ok?? (grin)

Many thanks, as always, to my family and friends for their love and support, you are always there for me...and I appreciate it!

Jamie Mills-Price
563 Taylor St. • Myrtle Creek, OR 97457 • phone: (541) 863-7933
info@betweenthevines.com • http://www.betweenthevines.com

© Copyright 2002 Jamie Mills-Price All rights reserved. Business or commercial use of any part of this publication is prohibited. Patterns and instructions are intended for the individual's fun or profit. Patterns may be reproduced for teaching purposes only. Patterns may be enlarged or reduced for personal use. No fee is to be charged. Reproduced patterns must contain the following: Book title, author's name(s) and the words "not for resale".

Disclaimer: The information in this book is presented in good faith. No warranty is given to the user relating to the material used in this book. Since we have no control over the physical conditions surrounding the application of the information contained herein, Jamie Mills-Price will not be liable for any untoward results, or charges made against the user for claims of patent or copyright infringement.

Would you like to meet people who share the same love of painting as you?
Become a member of The Society of Decorative Painters. For more information write:
The Society of Decorative Painters
393 N. McLean Blvd. • Wichita • KS 67203-5968

Distributed by: *Easl* ®
Essential Authors Services Ltd.
P.O. Box 22088 • St. Louis, MO • 63126
Phone: (314) 892-9222 • Fax: (314) 892-9607
Visit our web site at: http:\\www.easlpublications.com

Project Index

"Winter Wishes" 10-11
(barrel stave) (photo - inside front cover)

"Patriotic Gingerbread" 12-13
(round box) (photo - inside front cover)

"In the Meadow" 14-15
(candle holder) (photo - inside front cover
& page 33)

"Blizzard Buddies" 16-21
(wooden shovel)
(photo - front cover & inside front cover)

"Snow Folk" 21-23
(trio of ornaments) (photo - page 32)

"Sweet Snowmen" 24-25
(candle holders) (photo - page 32)

"Oh Snow Happy" 26-28
(tin bucket) (photo - page 32)

"Oh Christmas Tree" 29-30
(ornaments) (photo - page 32)

"Christmas Treasures" 35-38
(square box) (photo - page 32)

"Sweet Ginger Angel" 38-39
(wobbly angel) (photo - page 31)

"Homespun Christmas" 40-42
(box)(photo - page 31)

"Gingerbread Grins" 43-44
(mini sled ornaments) (photo - page 31)

"Midnight Twinkles" 45-46
(suds dipper pot) (photo - page 33)

"Tiny Treasures" 47-50
(framed plaque) (photo - page 33)

"Snowflake Tin" 50-52
(tin bowl) (photo - inside back cover)

"Trio of Wood Pots (twig hearts)...52-53
(wood pots) (photo - inside back cover)

"Trio of Wood Pots (snowmen)....53-54
(arch plaque) (photo - inside back cover)

"North Pole or Bust" 55-57
(wood basket) (photo - inside back cover)

"Snow Sweet Snow" 57-60
(wooden canister) (photo - back cover)

"Ring of Holly" 61-62
(bowl) (photo - back cover)

 # Supply List

Antique Maroon (160)
Antique Mauve (162)
Antique White (58)
Black Plum (172)
Burnt Orange (16)
Burnt Sienna (63)
Burnt Umber (64)
Buttermilk (3)
Camel (191)
Crimson Tide (21)
Deep Midnight Blue (166)
Driftwood (171)
Evergreen (82)
French Grey Blue (98)
French Mauve (186)
Gingerbread (218)
Jade Green (57)
Khaki Tan (173)
Light Avocado (106)
Light Buttermilk (164)
Light French Blue (185)
Mauve (26)
Midnight Green (85)
Milk Chocolate (174)
Mink Tan (92)
Mississippi Mud (94)
Moon Yellow (7)
Neutral Grey (95)
Payne's Grey (167)
Plantation Pine (113)
Raw Sienna (93)
Rookwood Red (97)
Sable Brown (61)
Slate Grey (68)
Soft Black (155)
Uniform Blue (86)

 # More Supplies

BRUSHES
Loew/Cornell
La Cornielle Golden Taklon
Series 7300 Shaders
   Nos. 14, 12, 10, 8, 6, 4, 2, 1, 0
Series 7050 Script Liners Nos. 1, 18/0
Series 7350 Liners Nos. 10/0
Series 7500 Filberts Nos. 8, 6, 4, 2, 10/0
Series 7550 Glaze/Wash 3/4, 1/2
Comfort Handle Brushes:
Series 3000 Rounds #3, 1, 00
DM Stippler Series Nos. 1/2, 3/8, 1/4, 1/8
Maxine's Mops Series 270 Nos. 3/4,
Maxine's Foam Edger Series 271

Loew/Cornell: 384 Brush Tub II
DES Double Ended Stylus
No. 80809-5 Grey Graphite
No. 80915-3 White Graphite
393 Super Chacopaper
No. 41-F Palette Knife
Better Way® Acrylic Brush Cleaning Fluid

General Painting Instructions

SHADING DOTS/LINES:

The dots/lines on my patterns designate where I have shaded the design, the darker the dots/lines get, the darker your shading should be...the lighter the dots, the lighter the shading is (and the color is walked out). Please refer to these inked dots for guidance on where to shade if it is not directly listed in the instructions.

WOOD PREP:

If the wood piece needs sanding, make sure that you sand with the grain of the wood. If you don't move with the grain of the wood, you will notice "scratches" on the wood. After sanding, remove the dust with a slightly dampened paper towel. After sealing, sand again and wipe free of dust.

❋ *TIP: As a final sand, I will use, "Super Film" an extremely fine sanding paper, (available through Houston Art & Frame) to get my surface nice and smooth.*

BASE-COAT:

This is your initial coat of paint. If you thin your paint with a little water, before you begin, you will have a smoother base-coat. It may take a little longer to achieve opaqueness, but your final result will be a beautiful surface to begin painting on. I usually sand lightly between coats, with Super Film.

❋ *TIP: The brush of my choice for base coating is a filbert. I have several different sizes that I really love, the #6, which is probably my most used for small areas and the large 1" are wonderful for varnishing.*

WASH:

Generally means a transparent coverage of paint. Adding water to your paint will thin it down; sometimes a glazing medium will achieve a smoother wash. The more water or medium you add, the lighter your color will be.

❋ *TIP: Err on the side of having your wash be too light, rather than too dark as it is easy to make it darker, but is much harder to make it lighter if you get it too dark!*

TRACING/TRANSFERRING YOUR PATTERN:

Trace your pattern onto tracing paper, with a pencil or pen. To transfer the pattern onto the surface, use graphite paper (which is removed by erasing) or Chaco-Paper (which is removed with water) and a stylus. Have a light touch as you transfer, so that you don't etch the design into the wood! I tend to use a lot of water when I paint, so I usually use graphite to transfer with, and I am careful to cover it when I basecoat.

❋ *TIP: Place a piece of waxed paper over the design as you transfer, so that you can see what part of the design you have traced over.*

BRUSH CARE:

It is important when you invest in good quality brushes, that you take excellent care of them. Never let a brush sit with paint in it.... Always wash the brush out after using it and as you are painting, if your brush gets too loaded up with paint. I also want to recommend the use of a brush basin. These hold water and they have grids in the bottom, which, will help prevent paint from building up in your brush. They are meant to be used gently, not pressed so hard against the grids that you damage the bristles.

❋ *TIP: The new, gray brush basins from Loew/Cornell are the best design I have seen yet, the grids are shaped/angled so that they don't break down the hair on one or the other side, of your brush, and it has a lid to cover it when transporting. Nice!*

Tips & Techniques

For best results, please read through these tips and refer to them when painting.

LOADING YOUR BRUSH - in preparation for floating color:

Step 1: When floating color, dip your flat brush fully into water, and blot briefly on a (lint-free) paper towel, until the shine disappears. Now place one corner only into the paint, getting a small amount on the brush. Move to your waxed palette, and blend…back and forth…applying PRESSURE, (to help blend the paint and the water together).

Step 2: Try to keep a straight, not curved, blending area…usually about a 1½"-2" long. Blend-blend-blend. You should see a nice graduation of color…fading to clear. It is important, that the edge that you kept free of paint stays clear. If you see color creep across to that side, you need to wash your brush, reload, and be more careful when you are blending, that the color does not stretch across your brush.

Step 3: Gently, pull your fingers (in a pinching manner) over the water corner of the brush, to remove excess moisture, before moving to your project.

FLOATING /SHADING/SIDE-LOADING/ TIPS:

Tip 1: Please refer to the inked dots on my patterns…to give you a general idea of where to float the shadows. It will help you if you can't tell from the photo.

Tip 2: First of all floating color takes practice…don't get discouraged, we all had to start somewhere!

Tip 3: Use the largest possible brush that you can for an area, to shade/highlight/glaze.

Tip 4: Layering your floats will give you a much softer, more dimensional effect. Rather than trying to achieve your depth in one application, which usually ends up looking harsh and too bold.

Tip 5: Pre-moistening the area that you want float with water, will usually make it easier to achieve a nice soft graduation of color.

Tip 6: Let your floats dry between layers, and accelerate the drying time if you need to, with a hair dryer.

Tip 7: Using a mop brush after you have floated your color will help to pick up any imperfections, and help to soften out your floats. As I stated in my last book, I have really come to like the new Maxine's Mops, they are made of soft, white goat hair, which makes it easy to see when they are dirty. They have tapered bristles, and lend themselves nicely to being able to mop vertically as well as horizontally.

Tip 8: When I mop, I begin in the water area and work in -towards the paint color. with a soft up and down motion, lightly mopping up any little imperfections.

Tip 9: Clean your mop brush often on a damp spot on your toweling to avoid the little specks that will appear, which is usually dried paint flakes. After cleaning, make sure you scrub out on a dry area of your towel to remove any moisture. It is supposed to be used DRY.

Tip 10: For more control…. Pull your floats toward your body, even if you have to move your project around. Using your pinky finger to anchor/stabilize your hand will help.

Tip 11: Get a container of "Wet Ones" (the kind with alcohol), they are wonderful for wiping off a mistake, even one that has dried out. Secondly, instant hand sanitizer (like Purell) is a great brush cleaner in a pinch, (and it even removes paint mistakes!).

Tip 12: Let me extol the virtues of having good quality brushes when you are painting. They are worth every penny! Your floating is only as good as your brushes. A lot of headaches can be avoided if you will invest in quality brushes. Learn from our mistakes, and begin with the best! I remember when I first began painting, I was using cheap craft brushes, did not "really" think it mattered about the quality…well, I remember one evening being really frustrated with my floating and then my teacher handed me one of her good brushes and let me float with it. I can tell you, it was like night and day!

Tip 13: Always clean your brushes out after each use, and never let them sit in the water in your brush basin. If you take care of them, they will last a long time. Store them with the hairs pointing upward, also.

GLAZING:

I use the term glazing throughout my instructions when I want to deposit just a light, sheer tint of color. It is not meant to change the color that it is placed over, just to enhance it.

Tip 1: I use the 1/2" or 3/4" Glaze/Wash brush when I do all my shading/highlighting/glazing techniques, and of course, a moistened brush.

Tip 2: Use a SMALL amount of color side-loaded in your brush, blend well on your palette and walk away from your blending area before moving to your project.

DOUBLE-LOADING:

This is achieved by loading a color on the corner of your brush, and another color on the opposite corner. They should meet in the middle. Blend on your palette, back and forth, until you have a nice graduation of color between the two.

TRIPLE-LOADING:

This is achieved by loading the brush fully into one color, blend on palette, now tip one corner in a color, and the opposite corner in another color. (You have three colors on your brush.) Now blend the triple-loaded brush on your palette, keeping the blending spot about a 1½"-2" long. If you are using a wet palette, this blending spot will stay wet for quite awhile.

STIPPLING:

Stippling can be done in a number of ways. You can use a deerfoot brush, an old scruffy brush, or my personal favorite, the DM Stipplers. Sea wool sponges can also be used to stipple. Load the brush of your choice with paint and pounce blend on your palette to distribute the paint through the bristles. You can also double and triple-load your Stipplers, to create multi-dimensional stippling.

DRY-BRUSHING:

I use this technique a lot in my style of painting. I almost exclusively use the DM Stipplers for all my dry-brushing, since the first time I grabbed one and used it, it has become my favorite brush for this, not as soft as an old scruffy brush, it has more body to it. I have two sets of these brushes, one I use for dry brushing and one I use for stippling!

Tip 1: Load the brush with a small amount of paint, swirl on your palette to distribute the color throughout the bristles...and then take to a dry area on your paper towel and scrub out most of the color.

Tip 2: As you dry-brush, use light pressure...gradually increase the pressure to deposit more color. *Use a light touch as it is so much easier to add color than to remove it if you get too much! For cheeks, I move the brush in a circular manner as I am softly scrubbing, for clothes I will either move the brush in a circular manner, or up and down depending on the area to fill.

BACK-TO-BACK FLOAT:

This is achieved by side-loading your brush, and laying down a float of color, and then flipping your brush over...and laying down a float, right next to it. So the paint edges are back to back, the water edges are out.

Tip 1: A lot of people find it easier to pre-moisten the area first with water, (before you float), and use a mop to soften the float out.

Tip 2: I usually will lay the repeat the stroke, over-stroking the initial deposit of color, as needed to adjust the quality.

LINEWORK:

I generally use script liners for my linework. (If you are just beginning to paint, you might want to start with a little shorter liner.) For more control...pull your linework toward you, (at least this works for me!) use your pinky finger to steady yourself. The paint consistency should be inky...the more pressure you use the thicker your lines will be.

GRAPEVINE/TWIGS:

I use vines to fill in a lot of the blank areas in my projects; this is my preference, (they are always an option, you can use them or leave them off...make yourself happy.) Load the liner in the color of choice; hold the brush in your hand, letting the brush rest on your middle finger...being held by your thumb. Now, drag the brush along...using a rocking motion, between these digits. Create squiggly, sharp...not rounded vinework. Use more pressure for thicker vines, and ease up for finer vines. Pulling your vinework toward you should help control it.

Tip 1: I always use script liners, and love the 7050 Series from Loew/Cornell.

Tip 2: The color of the vine will depend on the background, and the areas you will be placing the vine. If you are on a dark surface, then you will need to add a lighter color so that the vine will show up. If you are on a light surface, add a darker pigmented paint so that they show up well

EASY STROKE LEAVES:

Tip 1: I use flat brushes that have nice chisel edges for my stroke leaves.

Tip 2: With your brush moistened with water, load the brush in the color of your choice, and blend well on palette.

Tip 3: Think of an "S" stroke when doing these, you need to modify it, so it is not too "essey", more of a diamond shape.

Tip 4: Start on the chisel edge of the brush, flatten and pull back up on the chisel edge of the brush.

Tip 5: Pull your strokes away from the vine as you work.

WOODGRAINING:

Tip 1: Use flat brushes with nice, sharp chisel edges. Side-load the paint on the brush and blend well on the palette

Tip 2: Start on the chisel edge, pull down (or up, or sideways) and place your first float coming back onto the chisel edge. (Refer to the photo/pattern for design shape). I usually will place 4-5 consecutive floats one inside the other, gradually decreasing the size until you fade into nothing. Because you are placing each consecutive float down on water that you have laid from the previous float, the color will eventually fade into nothing…getting lighter and lighter as you decrease in size.

Tip 3: Have a mop brush handy, to soften up your floats, especially the end of the stroke.

SNOW EFFECTS:

I use a large brush side-loaded in Light Buttermilk (usually), blend well on your palette. Begin by floating directly under the objects with a circular (bumpy?) motion, flip the brush over and use the (clean) water edge to smooth and smear out the edges. I repeat this several times, until I have the desired opaqueness. I tend to make the color a bit brighter/bolder under the objects and soften (or taper off) away from that.

Tip 1: Use a mop brush to soften the outer edges if needed.

Sources

Treasures of the Heart
119 S. Old Pacific Hwy.
Myrtle Creek, OR 97457
(541) 863-4466
1-888-346-0614
treasuresoftheheart@hotmail.com

Smooth Cut Wood
PO Box 507
Aurora, OR 97002
(503) 678-1318
1-888-982-9663

Be Creative
174 Oakdale Road
North York, Ontario
Canada   M3N 2S5
(416) 742-8535 or (416) 742-5575
FAX: (416) 742-1842

Valhalla Designs
343 Twin Pines Drive
Glendale, OR 97442
(541) 832-3260 (phone / fax)
info@valhalladesigns.com
http://www.ValhallaDesigns.com

Painter's Paradise
111 Parrish Lane
Wilmington, Delaware 19810
(302) 478-7619 - Voice
(302) 478-9441 – Fax
jodecart@aol.com
http://www.paintersparadise.com

Viking Woodcrafts, Inc.
1317 8th St. SE
Waseca, MN 56093
(800) 328-0116 -Phone
(507) 835-3895 -Fax
viking@vikingwoodcrafts.com
http://www.vikingwoodcrafts.com

Stan Brown Arts & Crafts
13435 NE Whitaker Way
Portland, OR 97230
(800) 547-5531
sbrown4207@aol.com
http://www.stanbrownartsand crafts.com

Bear with Us
3007 S. Kendall Ave.
Independence, MO 64055
(816) 373- 3231
Email: BEARWJS@aol.com

Cape Cod Cooperage
1150 Queen Anne Rd.
Chatham, MA 02633
(508) 432-0788

# "Winter Wishes"

(Barrel Stave) (color photo - inside front cover)

"Here is another barrel stave for your Christmas collection, I enjoy painting on these staves...they make great gifts and/or for holiday bazaars. Happy Painting!"

Surface/Supplier:
"Cape Cod Cooperage" 14" barrel stave
Smooth Cut Wood
PO Box 507
Aurora, OR 97002
(503) 678-1318

Palette:
Deco Art Americana

Antique White	Burnt Umber
Deep Midnight Blue	Gingerbread
Light Buttermilk	Plantation Pine
Rookwood Red	Soft Black

Brushes:
Loew/Cornell Golden Taklon
Series 7300 Shaders No. 16, 6, 1
Series 7050 Script Liners No. 10/0
Series 7000 Rounds No. 3
Series 270 Maxine's Mops No. 1/2,

INSTRUCTIONS

Sand, seal and sand again. Base with a 2:1 mix of Deep Midnight Blue/Soft Black.
(If a brighter blue is desired then don't mix with the Soft Black.)

INITIAL BASE-COATS

Snowman: Antique White
Heart and two leaves: Antique White
Lettering: Antique White, #1 flat.
Checkerboard: Antique White, #6 flat, stitches are Antique White.

Snowman:
Step 1: Shade with Burnt Umber, along the R side and under each level. Highlight with Light Buttermilk on the L side of the body.
Step 2: Apply pattern, and stroke the arms on with the #3 round, loaded in Burnt Umber and stroked through Antique White.

Eyes: Soft Black, highlight with Light Buttermilk.
Nose: Gingerbread, while wet...stroke Burnt Umber across the bottom and Antique White across the top.
Cheeks: Dry-Brush with Rookwood Red, highlight with a dot of Light Buttermilk.
Mouth: Soft Black, glaze the lower lip with Rookwood Red.
Wreath on Head: Line and add leaves with Plantation Pine, the berries are Rookwood Red.
Vines: With a liner and Burnt Umber, stroke the vine on, pull through Antique White as needed to highlight. The leaves are Plantation Pine (#6 flat), side-loaded in Antique White when needing a brighter leaf. The berries are Rookwood Red, using a stylus.
Heart: Shade the top with Rookwood Red, and highlight the bottom with Light Buttermilk. The 2 leaves are shaded with Plantation Pine, and highlighted with Light Buttermilk. Dot Light Buttermilk under heart. Add fine vines with a brush mix of Plantation Pine and Antique White.

FINISHING DETAILS

Float under the snowman with Antique White; float the edges of the stave over the checks with Burnt Umber. Spatter Burnt Umber over snowman body. I finished the back with the same color as the front. Erase all remaining graphite lines, and varnish. Enjoy!

"Warm Winter Wishes"

"Winter Wishes"

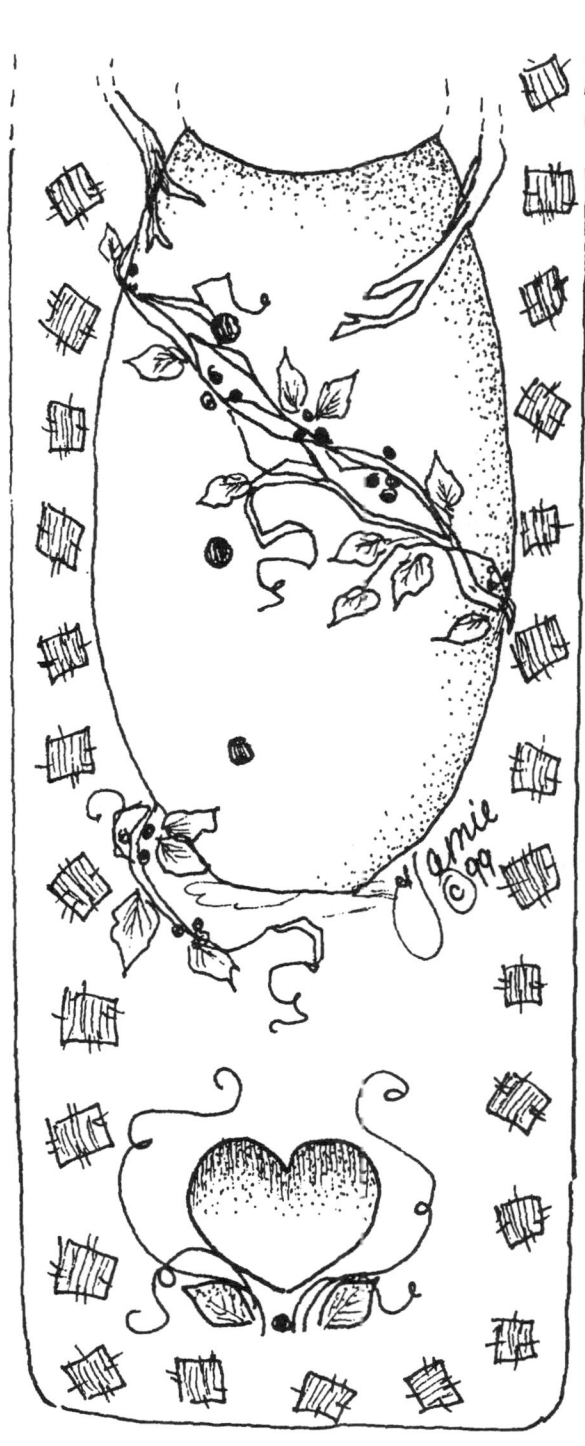

"Patriotic Gingerbread"

(Round Box) (color photo - inside front cover)

"This chunky little fellow is happy just sitting on his Americana birdhouse. For painters in other countries you could substitute your flag for ours, or make the stars into hearts, or you could just paint the house in one solid color. Enjoy!".

Surface/Supplier:
Round Box w/lid -small
Smooth Cut Wood
PO Box 507
Aurora, OR 97002
(503) 678-1318

Palette:
Deco Art Americana
Black Plum
Buttermilk
Deep Midnight Blue
Light Buttermilk
Mississippi Mud
Plantation Pine
Rookwood Red
Soft Black
Hot Shots Fiery Red

Burnt Umber
Camel
Khaki Tan
Mink Tan
Payne's Grey
Raw Sienna
Sable Brown

Brushes:
Loew/Cornell Golden Taklon
Series 7550 Glaze/Wash No. 3/4, 1/2
Series 7300 Shaders Nos. 6, 4
Series 7050 Script Liners No. 18/0
Series DM Stipplers No. 1/8, 3/8
Series Maxine Mops Nos. 3/4, 1/2

Misc. Supplies:
American Traditional Brass Stencil: Stars, Hearts and Dots

INSTRUCTIONS

Step 1: Sand, seal and sand again. Base the lid in Khaki Tan; base the side of the box in Deep Midnight Blue; base the lower lip in Khaki Tan. Band the top and bottom edges in Rookwood Red.

Step 2: Apply the pattern and base as follows:

INITIAL BASECOATS

Gingerbread Man: Sable Brown
Birdhouse Roof: Camel
House: Buttermilk; Red stripes are Rookwood Red; Union is Deep Midnight Blue; Door is Sable Brown; Hole is Soft Black.

SHADING AND DETAIL

Note: Float around the Gingerbread Man and the house, with soft floats of Mississippi Mud. Deepen in the darkest areas with Burnt Umber. Float around the perimeter of the lid and box with Mississippi Mud, and drybrush in the open areas (stay out of the shadows) with Buttermilk.

Gingerbread Man:

Step 1: Apply the pattern as needed.
Step 2: Shade the Gingerbread man with Burnt Umber, highlight with Mink Tan.
Step 3: The features are Soft Black, except the nose, which is Rookwood Red. The frosting and buttons are Buttermilk. The cheeks are drybrushed on with Rookwood Red. Shade the buttons and the frosting with Burnt Umber. Shade under the frosting and buttons with Burnt Umber, so that they appear dimensional.
Step 4: Add highlights in the eyes, cheeks and nose with Buttermilk.

Birdhouse-
Roof:
Step 1: Shade the backside with Raw Sienna, deepen with Burnt Umber. Highlight the lower edge with Buttermilk.

House:
Step 1: Stencil the stars on with Buttermilk. Shade the union, under the roof edge, with Payne's Grey. Highlight next to the stripe edge with Buttermilk.
Step 2: The red stripes are shaded with Black Plum on the outer edges, and highlighted on the

inside edges with Hot Shots Fiery Red. The white stripes are shaded on the outer edges with Mississippi Mud, deepened with Burnt Umber and highlighted on the inside edges with Light Buttermilk.

Step 3: Float a side-load of Burnt Umber down the Left side of the union to antique it a bit.

Step 4: The vines around the union are stroked on with Burnt Umber tipped in Buttermilk, as needed to highlight, (18/0 liner). Add a highlight in the hole with Buttermilk; the perch is Soft Black.

Door:

Step 1: Shade the top and bottom with Burnt Umber; add woodgrain with Burnt Umber. Highlight the sides of the door with Mink Tan, and highlight some of the woodgrain edges with Mink Tan.

Step 2: The door has a line of Burnt Umber down the Right side. The hinges are Soft Black, and the heart handle is Buttermilk.

Vines and Leaves:

Step 1: The vines are stroked on with Burnt Umber tipped in Buttermilk as desired to highlight.

Step 2: The leaves are Plantation Pine, using the #4 flat.

Snow:

Step 1: Side load Buttermilk on the 1/2" flat and float the snow on in soft layers. Highlight further with Light Buttermilk, more in toward the front of the house. *I like the effect of having transparent mounds fading away into the background, so those would be the Buttermilk color.

FINISHING DETAILS

Step 1: Check the edges of the lid and box with Deep Midnight Blue using the #6 flat. Dots between are Buttermilk. Spatter over the box with Burnt Umber.

Step 2: The stars on the sides of the box are stenciled with Buttermilk; when dry...float over the Left sides of the stars with Burnt Umber.

Step 3: Erase any remaining graphite and varnish as desired. Enjoy!

"Patriotic Gingerbread"

"In the Meadow"

(Candle Holder) (color photo - inside front cover & page 33)

"This jolly snowman has his arms up and open wide to welcome his friends into the meadow. Have fun painting him for winter!"

Surface/Supplier:
(Provo Craft) Snowman
Treasures of the Heart
119 S, Old Pacific Hwy.
Myrtle Creek, OR 97457
(541) 863-4466
treasuresoftheheart@hotmail.com

Palette:
Deco Art Americana

Burnt Orange	Burnt Umber
Buttermilk	Camel
Deep Midnight Blue	Evergreen
French Grey Blue	Jade Green
Khaki Tan	Light Buttermilk
Mauve	Mississippi Mud
Raw Sienna	Rookwood Red
Soft Black	

Brushes:
Loew/Cornell Golden Taklon
Series 7550 Wash/Glaze No. 3/4, 1/2
Series 7300 Shaders No. 6, 2, 1
Series 7050 Script Liners No. 18/0
Series DM Stipplers No. 3/8
Series Maxine's Mop No. 1/2

INSTRUCTIONS

Step 1: Sand, seal and sand again.
Step 2: Base the snowman's face, neckband, lower body section, hat brim and round base in Buttermilk. Base the snowman's middle section in Deep Midnight Blue. Base the top of the hat in Khaki Tan and the hatband in Rookwood Red.
Step 3: The hearts are Rookwood Red.

INITIAL BASECOATS

 **Note:** The back scene section of the snowman is repeated with the front design.

Step 1: Apply the patterns for the separate scenes, and base all the snowmen in Light Buttermilk. On the front panel, base the birdhouses (L-R): Mauve; French Grey Blue with Camel roof; Jade Green. All of the posts and holes are Soft Black. The rooftops and bases on the Mauve and Jade Green birdhouse are Soft Black.

SHADING AND DETAIL

Snowman Spindle:
Step 1: The eyes, brows, mouth are Soft Black. The cheeks are dry-brushed on with Rookwood Red; float the lip with Rookwood Red. Add a highlight in the eyes and cheeks with Light Buttermilk. The nose (which is wire) is lightly painted with Burnt Orange.
Step 2: Underneath the chin, stripe the section with Rookwood Red, using the #6 flat. Shade under the chin with Burnt Umber.
Step 3: Underneath the blue middle section, float Mississippi Mud. Check around the scene sections with Deep Midnight Blue, using the #6 flat.
Step 4: The blue middle section has lettering of Light Buttermilk; softly float over the bottoms of the letters with Burnt Umber.
Step 5: The hearts are highlighted with Buttermilk.
Step 6: The hat has checks of Deep Midnight Blue along the edge, using the #2 flat. Add vines on top of the brim with Burnt Umber, stroke leaves on with Evergreen, using the #1 flat. The Rookwood Red hatband is left as is. The top of the hat has stripes of Burnt Umber using the #4 flat. Shade with Burnt Umber above the red hatband, and highlight right next to the brass candle ring.

Scenes:
(L-R: Left side; Front; and Right side. Again, the back section is a repeat of the front.)

All Vines:
Step 1: With inky (water added) Burnt Umber and the 18/0 liner, stroke the vines on. At the waist,

add leaves to the vines with Evergreen and the #1 flat.

Step 2: Float around the vines (here and there) with Mississippi Mud and then with washy French Grey Blue. At the waist, float Burnt Umber under the blue section.

All Snowmen/scenes:

Step 1: Shade snowmen with Mississippi Mud, float along the bottoms with French Grey Blue. Float around the snowmen and the snow mounds with Mississippi Mud.

Step 2: The arms are stroked on with Burnt Umber.

Step 3: The eyes, mouth, buttons and stitches are Soft Black. The noses are Burnt Orange.

Left Side:

Step 1: Left side has no special detail, just the snowmen.

Front:

Step 1: The birdhouses (L-R)- Shade the Mauve house with Rookwood Red; add grain lines with Soft Black. Shade the blue house with Deep Midnight Blue; add grain lines with Soft Black. The roof is shaded and has strokes of, Raw Sienna. Highlight along the front edge of Buttermilk. The green house is shaded with Evergreen, highlighted with Light Buttermilk. Add grain lines of Soft Black.

Right Side:

Step 1: The broom is the only special detail on the Right side; the broom itself is stroked on with Raw Sienna, with a Burnt Umber handle and separation.

Round Base:

Step 1: Check the base with Rookwood Red, using the #6 flat. Add a fir bough garland, (just above the checks): Stroke Burnt Umber on with the 18/0 liner and add the needles with Evergreen.

FINISHING DETAILS

Step 1: Spatter with Burnt Umber and then Buttermilk. Erase any remaining graphite, and varnish as desired.

"In the Meadow"

IN THE MEADOW WE CAN BUILD A SNOWMAN!

"Blizzard Buddies"

(Wooden Shovel) (color photo - front cover & inside front cover)

Thanks go to Don at Valhalla Designs for this wonderful shovel! I just love to paint for Winter (hence this book...) and I think these cozy, winter friends all snuggled up against one another will have no problem keeping warm during the blizzard. Paint this large shovel and prop it up next to your fireplace or hang it on the wall. Instead of a dark blue crackled background, you could try a dark green or even burgundy would look great. Happy Painting!"

Surface/Supplier:
Item # S-31 Shovel
Valhalla Designs
343 Twin Pines Drive
Glendale, OR 97442
(541) 832-3260
http://www.ValhallaDesigns.com

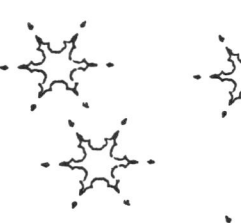

Palette:
Deco Art Americana
Antique White
Burnt Umber
Camel
Evergreen
Jade Green
Light Buttermilk
Midnight Green
Neutral Grey
Raw Sienna
Slate Grey
Hot Shots Fiery Red

Black Plum
Buttermilk
Deep Midnight Blue
French Grey Blue
Khaki Tan
Mauve
Mississippi Mud
Payne's Grey
Rookwood Red
Soft Black

Brushes:
Loew/Cornell Golden Taklon
Series 7550 Glaze/Wash No. 3/4, 1/2
Series 7300 Shaders No. 1, 2, 8
Series 7050 Script Liners No. 4, 18/0
Series DM Stipplers No. 1/8, 1/4, 1/2
Series Maxine's Mop No. 3/4, 1/2

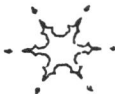

Misc. Supplies:
Deco Art Weathered Wood
Deco Art Snowtex

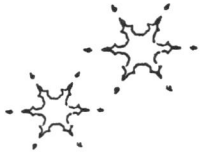

INSTRUCTIONS

❄ **Option:** If you so desire, you could eliminate some of the detail of this project, by leaving the mouse and cat out of the design, just round out the snowman's body and the wreath.

Step 1: Sand, seal and sand again. Base entire shovel and handle in Khaki Tan.

Step 2: Apply the oval pattern outline as a guide for crackling around the inset. Brush the crackle medium on the shovel and on the handle, and let dry according to manufacturers instructions.

❄ **Tip:** Don't be concerned about making too fine an edge along the inset with the crackle medium, as the vines will hide any imperfections.

Step 3: Apply the topcoat of Deep Midnight Blue; use very little water and a large brush. Let dry well. *Again, don't be too concerned about creating a fine, even edge with the topcoat, as the vines around the inset will cover a multitude of imperfections.

Step 4: Apply the pattern for the inset scene and basecoat as follows.

INITIAL BASECOATS

Snowman's Body: Buttermilk
Hat: Soft Black
Holly and Berries: Holly is Jade Green; Berries are Mauve.
Scarf: Base entirely in Buttermilk, and then add the red stripes with a dark wash of Rookwood Red.
Coat: Deep Midnight Blue
Buttons of Coal: Soft Black
Flag: The union is Deep Midnight Blue; the white and red section are based first in Buttermilk, then the red section is washed with Rookwood Red.
Flag Pole: Mississippi Mud
Mouse: Slate Grey
Mouse Dress: Jade Green; Yoke and trim is Antique White.
Cat: Camel

Cat Dress: Sleeves are French Grey Blue; Bodice is Mauve; skirt is Antique White.

❄ Bluebirds will be based in later, after the majority of the scene is painted. The wreath is not based in either it is stippled on.

SHADING AND DETAIL

❄ Float around objects and oval edge with Mississippi Mud and deepen softly with Burnt Umber. Drybrush with Buttermilk in the open areas of the background.

Snowman:

Step 1: Apply the pattern for features and pipe. Base the eyes, lashes, and mouth in Soft Black. The nose is Mauve; the pipe is Camel and the stem is Mississippi Mud.

Step 2: Shade the snowman first with Khaki Tan, deepen with soft floats of Mississippi Mud. Highlight with Light Buttermilk and float a very soft side-load glaze of color down the Left side of the snowman's body with Payne's Grey. *Walk this color out on your palette, until it is very sheer.

Step 3: Drybrush the cheeks on with Rookwood Red; float Rookwood Red on the lower lip and the bottom of the nose. Highlight in the cheeks, eyes and nose is Light Buttermilk.

Step 4: The pipe is lined and shaded with Raw Sienna, and highlighted with Antique White around the opening. Fill in the area of the pipe that is coming directly out of his mouth and inside the bowl, with Soft Black.

Step 5: The hair (*paint after finishing the hat*) is stroked on with Burnt Umber and tipped in Mississippi Mud as it goes over the hat.

Step 6: The buttons are highlighted with Light Buttermilk; make sure you have shaded under the buttons using the shade colors.

Hat:

Step 1: The hat is floated with Slate Grey; highlight the brim with Light Buttermilk.

Step 2: The holly is lined and shaded with Evergreen, deepen with Midnight Green. Highlight with a brush mix of Jade Green and Light Buttermilk. The berries are shaded with Rookwood Red, and highlight with Buttermilk.

Scarf:

Step 1: Shade the white stripes with Mississippi Mud; highlight with Light Buttermilk. Shade the red stripes with Black Plum; highlight with Hot Shots Fiery Red. *Float back over the Hot Shots highlight with a side-load of Rookwood Red, to tone down the color if desired.

Step 2: The fringe is stroked on with the 18/0 liner, Rookwood Red and Buttermilk.

Coat:

Step 1: Apply the pattern for the snowmen, moon, trees, and snow slopes. Shade the coat with Payne's Grey and highlight with Light Buttermilk. Drybrush with Light Buttermilk in the open areas of the coat.

Step 2: Base the snowmen in Light Buttermilk; shade with Mississippi Mud. The eyes/mouth/buttons are Soft Black. Noses are Raw Sienna. Twig arms are Antique White tipped in Mississippi Mud.

Step 3: The trees have trunks stroked on with Mississippi Mud and the limbs are Jade Green.

Step 4: The moon is shaded with Raw Sienna; shade under it with Payne's Grey.

Flag:

Step 1: The union has Buttermilk hearts; shade over the Right side with Burnt Umber. Highlight the Left side with Buttermilk.

Step 2: The red section has plaid linework of Black Plum, shade Black Plum and highlight with Buttermilk.

Step 3: The white section has linework of Mississippi Mud, shaded with Burnt Umber and highlighted with Light Buttermilk. Stitch with Soft Black.

Step 4: The flagpole is shaded and lined with Burnt Umber; highlight with Antique White; the ties are Antique White, with an overstroke of Light Buttermilk through the center.

Wreath:

Step 1: With the 1/8" DM stippler, double-load in Jade and Evergreen, tap blend on your palette and then stipple the wreath. Re-load your brush in Jade and Evergreen, and then side-load the Jade edge into Light Buttermilk and stipple

(continued on page 20)

"Blizzard Buddies"

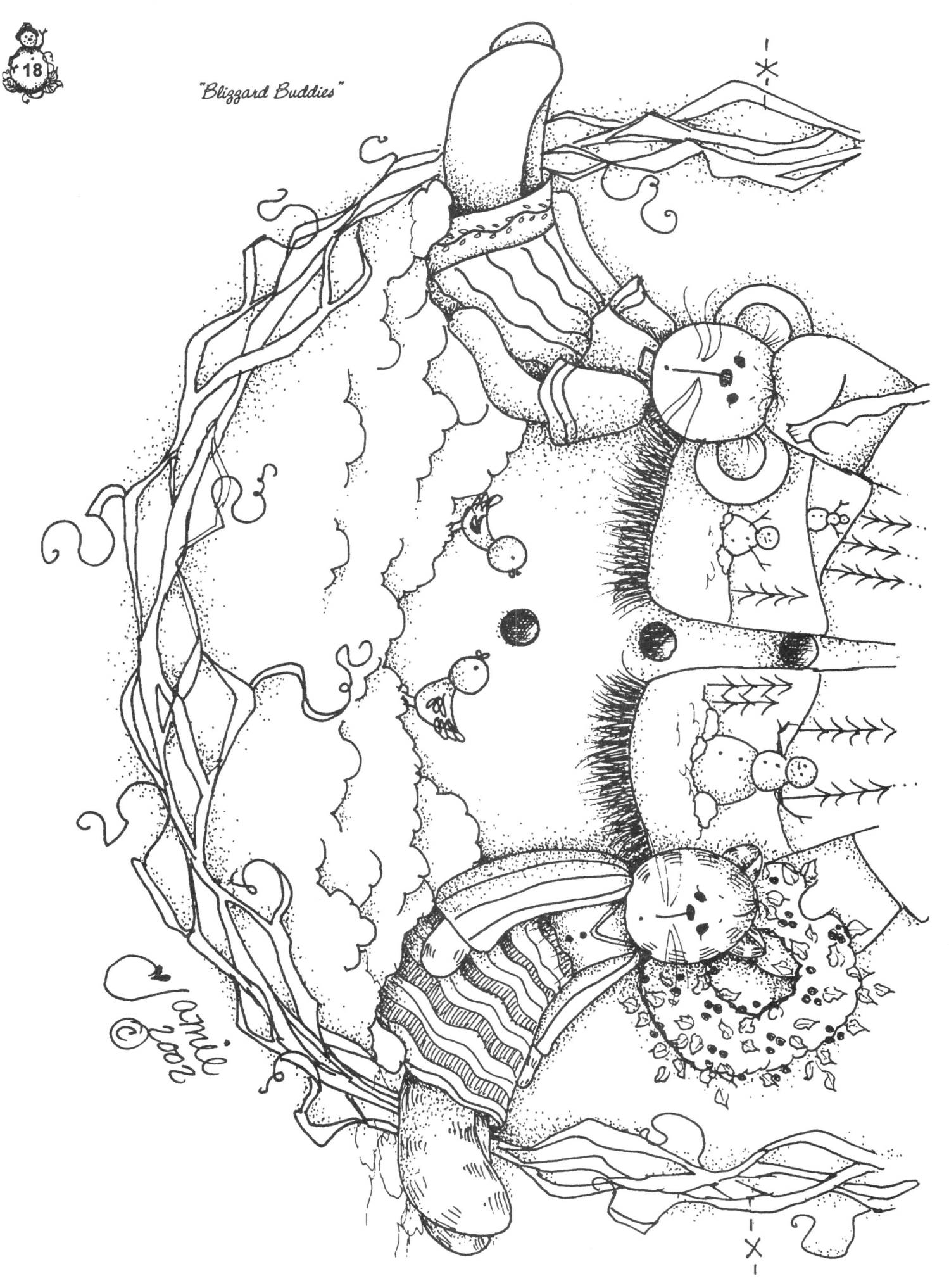

(continued from page 17)
back over the wreath. Shade with Evergreen around the hand and cat's head; deepen shading with Midnight Green.

Step 2: The little stroke leaves are Midnight Green, using the #1 flat. The berries are Rookwood Red.

"Buford" the Mouse:

Step 1: Shade with Neutral Grey; deepen with Soft Black and highlight with Light Buttermilk. Float in ears with Mauve and then Rookwood Red. The hair in the ears is Light Buttermilk. The hair on the head is Soft Black.

Step 2: The features are Soft Black, except the nose, which is Mauve. Shade the bottom of the nose with Rookwood Red. Dry-brush the cheeks on with Rookwood Red. Highlights in the eyes, nose and cheeks are Light Buttermilk. The whiskers are Light Buttermilk.

Step 3: The dress sleeves and skirt are lined with Evergreen, shaded with Evergreen and deepened with Midnight Green. Highlight with Light Buttermilk. The hem and bodice are shaded with Mississippi Mud, highlight with Buttermilk. Line the vine on the hem, the collar and along the bottom of the hem, with Midnight Green, add leaves (18/0 liner) on the hem and buttons on the collar with Rookwood Red.

"Hannah" the Cat:
This little cat was named after a student (friend)l Hannah Atkinson, I met her while travel teaching in Florid. She is wild about cats! (Especially sweet little Buford, aka. Mouse.)

Step 1: Stripe Hannah the Cat with a liner and Raw Sienna, shade with Raw Sienna and deepen with Burnt Umber, highlight with Buttermilk. The hair is Burnt Umber, tipped in Antique White.

Step 2: The features are Soft Black, except the nose, which is Mauve. Shade the bottom of the nose with Rookwood Red. Dry-brush the cheeks with Rookwood Red. Highlights in the eyes, nose and cheeks are Light Buttermilk. The whiskers are Light Buttermilk.

Step 3: The dress sleeves are lined and shaded Deep Midnight Blue; deepen shading with Payne's Grey and highlight with Light Buttermilk. The bodice is shaded with Rookwood Red, and highlighted with Light Buttermilk. Line with Light Buttermilk. Buttons are Rookwood Red.

Step 4: The skirt has stripes of Mississippi Mud, using the #2 flat. Line in between the stripes with Deep Midnight Blue. Shade with Mississippi Mud, deepen with Burnt Umber and highlight with Light Buttermilk.

Birds:

Step 1: The birds are based in French Grey Blue; shade with Payne's Grey and highlight with Light Buttermilk. Add feathers with Light Buttermilk and the 18/0 liner. The eyes are Soft Black, with a tiny dot at the back of Light Buttermilk. The beak is Raw Sienna and the feet/legs are Soft Black.

Vines:

Step 1: Make inky puddles (add water) of Antique White and Burnt Umber. Using the #4 script liner, load in Burnt Umber and pull through Antique White and stroke the vines around the oval. By adding pressure as you pull, you will have a thicker vine and lift up and get on the tip of the brush for finer vines. Finish off the vine with curly-Q's, using the 18/0 liner for a fine effect, and the same colors as the vine.

Step 2: Shade around the vine (on the inside) with Mississippi Mud and deepen with Burnt Umber. Shade around the vines (on the outside) with Payne's Grey.

Snow:

Step 1: Begin floating the snow on with Buttermilk, starting at the bottom of the snowman and sweeping downward. *Use a mop brush to soften the strokes and also the water edge of the brush to help smooth/smear the strokes out. Really build up this color, before moving to Light Buttermilk to finish brightening the tops of the mounds. If desired, you can softly float behind some of the mounds with Mississippi Mud.

❄ Make sure you pull some of the snow effects out over the vines and edges of the oval, around the animals.

Woodgrain:

Step 1: Create the woodgrain on the sides/back of the shovel and handle with a brush mix of Mississippi Mud and Burnt Umber. Highlight some of the graining with Antique White.

FINISHING DETAILS

Step 1: Add Snow Tex for special dimensional effects, mainly on the highest points of the snow peaks.

Step 2: Check the edge of the shovel with Deep Midnight Blue, using the #8 flat. The dots in between are Rookwood Red.

Step 2: Spatter with Light Buttermilk, using an old toothbrush or your favorite method.

Step 3: Erase any remaining graphite, and varnish as desired. Happy shoveling!

"Snow Folk"

(Trio of Ornaments) (color photo - page 32)

"I loved these puffy snowmen, they will look so sweet hanging on your tree...you could also reduce the pattern and create delightful little holiday pins. Have fun!"

Surface/Supplier:
"Bear with Us" Puffy Snowmen
Treasures of the Heart
119 S. Old Pacific Hwy.
Myrtle Creek, OR 97457
(541) 863-4466
treasuresoftheheart@hotmail.com

Palette:
Deco Art Americana

Black Plum	Burnt Orange
Burnt Umber	Buttermilk
Camel	Deep Midnight Blue
Evergreen	French Grey Blue
French Mauve	Jade Green
Khaki Tan	Light Buttermilk
Mauve	Midnight Green
Mississippi Mud	Payne's Grey
Raw Sienna	Rookwood Red
Soft Black	

Brushes:
Loew/Cornell Golden Taklon
Series 7550 Glaze/Wash No. 1/2
Series 7050 Script Liners No. 18/0
Series 7000 Rounds No. 3
Series DM Stipplers No. 1/4
Series Maxine Mops Nos. 1/2

INSTRUCTIONS
Step 1: Sand, seal and sand again.
Step 2: Apply the pattern for the individual snowmen, eliminating the detail.

INITIAL BASECOATS
Snowmen Faces/Bodies: Buttermilk
Blue Snowman:
   Hat - Deep Midnight Blue; **Brim**- French Grey Blue.
   Holly - Jade Green
   Vest - French Grey Blue
Green Snowman:
   Hat - Evergreen; **Brim**- Jade Green
   Vest - Evergreen; **Collar**- Jade Green
   Star/buttons on vest - Camel
Mauve Snowman:
   Hat - Mauve; **Brim**- Khaki Tan
   Shirt - Khaki Tan
   Apron - Mauve

SHADING AND DETAIL
All Snowmen:
Step 1: Shade with Mississippi Mud and deepen with Burnt Umber. Float a glaze (soft side-load) of Deep Midnight Blue down the Left side of the snow bodies. *Make this very, very soft...by walking out your color on the palette before floating. Highlight with Light Buttermilk on the chins, arms and bottoms of the bellies.
Step 2: Apply the pattern for the faces and fill in the

(continued on page 22)

(continued from page 21)

features with Soft Black-except for the noses, which on the green and pink snowmen are Burnt Orange, and on the blue snowman is Mauve.

Step 3: Drybrush the cheeks with Rookwood Red. Float the bottoms of the carrot noses with Burnt Umber and the pink nose with Rookwood Red. Highlight the tops of the noses, and the eyes and the cheeks with Light Buttermilk. Float Rookwood Red on the lips.

Step 4: The hair is stroked on with Burnt Umber tipped in Buttermilk...only AFTER you have painted their respective hats.

Blue Snowman:

Step 1: The hat brim and the vest are lined with Light Buttermilk, shaded with Deep Midnight Blue and deepened with Payne's Grey. Highlight with Light Buttermilk. Line the edges of the vest with Light Buttermilk, dot the buttons and add buttonholes with Light Buttermilk also. The fringe is Deep Midnight Blue. The top part of the hat is shaded with Payne's Grey, and drybrush a highlight of Light Buttermilk through the center area of the hat.

Step 2: The holly is floated with Evergreen, and highlighted with Light Buttermilk. The vein lines are Evergreen; the berries are Mauve with a highlight of Light Buttermilk.

Step 3: The buttons on the snowman are Mauve, shaded on the bottoms with Rookwood Red and highlighted on the tops with Light Buttermilk. Shade underneath the buttons with Mississippi Mud.

Green Snowman:

Step 1: The brim and collar are dotted with Evergreen, shaded with Evergreen and highlighted with Light Buttermilk. Line the collar with Light Buttermilk.

Step 2: The top part of the hat and the vest are both striped with Light Buttermilk. Shade with Midnight Green, and drybrush a highlight with Jade Green. Float Jade Green down the front placket of the vest. Stitch with Light Buttermilk.

Step 3: The star on the hat is floated on the bottom with Raw Sienna, highlighted on the top with Light Buttermilk. Add a dot in the center with Light Buttermilk. The twig effect is stroked on with Camel and then floated over with Raw Sienna.

Step 4: The buttons on the vest are shaded on the bottom with Raw Sienna, highlighted with Light Buttermilk on the top. The connecting string between is Raw Sienna tipped in Camel.

Step 5: The two buttons on the snowman are Soft Black, highlight with Light Buttermilk. Shade under them with Mississippi Mud.

Mauve Snowman:

Step 1: The hat brim and shirt are woven with Mississippi Mud to look like a sweater. *I take it row by row, working from side to side. Shade with Burnt Umber, highlight with a drybrush of Light Buttermilk through the center of the shirt and along the top of the brim and down the sides of the arms.

Step 2: Stitch, line and add buttons with Light Buttermilk.

Step 3: The upper hat and the apron are lined with French Mauve and Black Plum. Shade with Rookwood Red, and deepen with Black Plum. Highlight with French Mauve.

Step 4: The apron is lined and stitched with Light Buttermilk, add a button at the shoulder with Light Buttermilk.

Step 5: The hearts are based in Jade Green, shaded along the bottom with Evergreen and highlighted on the top with Light Buttermilk. The dots and stitches are added last with Light Buttermilk.

Step 6: The button on the snowman is Soft Black, highlighted with Light Buttermilk. Shade under with Mississippi Mud.

FINISHING DETAILS

Step 1: Erase any remaining graphite, varnish as desired.

Step 2: To hang the ornament, you can either drill a hole for hanging...or use a small screw eye and ribbon. Enjoy!

 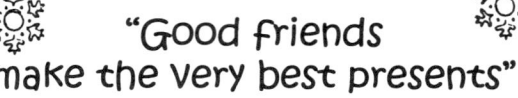

"Good friends make the very best presents"

"Snow Folk"

"Sweet Snowmen" candle holder

23

"Sweet Snowmen"

(Candle holders) (color photo - page 32)

"This pair of candleholders was so fun to paint, they would look great in your winter decorating plans...or for fun, leave them out year round."

Surface/Supplier:
"Bear With Us" Snowmen Candleholders
Treasures of the Heart
119 S. Old Pacific Hwy.
Myrtle Creek, OR 97457
(541) 863-4466
treasuresoftheheart@hotmail.com

Palette:
Deco Art Americana

Burnt Umber	Buttermilk
Deep Midnight Blue	Evergreen
French Grey Blue	Jade Green
Khaki Tan	Light Buttermilk
Mauve	Mississippi Mud
Rookwood Red	Soft Black

Brushes:
Loew/Cornell Golden Taklon
Series 7550 Glaze/Wash No. 3/4, 1/2
Series 7300 Shaders No. 6, 4, 1
Series 7050 Script Liners No.18/0
Series DM Stipplers 1/4
Series Maxine's Mops No. 1/2

INSTRUCTIONS/INITIAL BASECOATS

Step 1: Sand, seal and sand again.

Step 2: Basecoat the Snowmen body sections in Buttermilk. The round base on the tall spindle is Evergreen and on the short spindle is Deep Midnight Blue.

Step 3:

Tall Snowman's Hat: Brim is Evergreen; band is Mauve; top is Jade Green

Tall Snowman's Birdhouses: (L-R) French Grey Blue; Mauve; Jade, the rooftops and holes are Soft Black.

Short Snowman's Hat: Brim is Deep Midnight Blue; band is Khaki Tan; top part is French Grey Blue.

Short Snowman's Birdhouses: (L-R) Mauve; Khaki Tan; Jade Green, the rooftops and holes are Soft Black.

SHADING AND DETAIL

Snowmen (both):

Step 1: Check between the layers with the #4 flat and French Grey Blue. Shade with Mississippi Mud under the hats and over the checks. Further shade with Mississippi Mud around the birdhouses on the tall spindle, and along the bottom edge of the short spindle.

Step 2: Apply the patterns for the twig wreath buttons, and stroke the twigs on with Mississippi Mud and then over-stroke with soft (washy) Burnt Umber. Softly float around the twigs with Mississippi Mud. *Instructions for individual buttons are given below with the specific snowman.

Step 3: Apply the pattern for the faces and fill in with Soft Black, except for the noses with are Rookwood Red. The cheeks are dry-brushed on with Rookwood Red; add a highlight in the eyes, nose and cheeks with Light Buttermilk.

Tall Snowman:

Step 1: The twig buttons are lined and shaded with Deep Midnight Blue -for the top button, and with Evergreen -for the bottom button. Highlight the tops of the buttons with Light Buttermilk. Add buttonholes and thread with Soft Black.

Step 2: The top section of the hat is shaded above the hatband with Evergreen, and highlighted with Buttermilk at the top. The trees have trunks and limbs of Burnt Umber, with 'needles' stroked on with Evergreen.

Step 3: The hatband is shaded along the bottom with Rookwood Red, and highlighted across the top with Light Buttermilk. Add Light Buttermilk linework and dots.

Float a highlight on the front of the brim with Buttermilk.

Birdhouses (L-R)

Step 4: The blue birdhouse is shaded with Deep Midnight Blue; add grain lines from the roof with Soft Black. Highlight with Light Buttermilk on the house and add Light Buttermilk highlights in the holes of the house.

Step 5: The mauve birdhouse is shaded with Rookwood Red; add grain lines from the roof with Soft Black. Highlight with Light Buttermilk on the house and add Light Buttermilk highlights in the star hole.

Step 6: The green birdhouse is shaded with Evergreen; add grain lines from the roof with Soft Black. Highlight the house with Light Buttermilk, and add Light Buttermilk highlights in the heart holes.

Step 7: The vines are stroked on with the 18/0 liner loaded in Burnt Umber and pulled through Khaki Tan. Softly float here and there along the vine with Mississippi Mud. Add stroke leaves with Evergreen, using the #4 flat.

Step 8: Add small checks along the round base with Jade Green and the #1 flat. Place strokes along the edge of the base by fully loading the #6 flat in Jade Green and side loading in Plantation Pine. Place a dot of Mauve between each stroke.

Short Snowman:

Step 1: The star twig button is striped and shaded with Deep Midnight Blue and highlighted with Light Buttermilk at the top. The buttonholes and thread are Soft Black.

Step 2: The trees along the bottom of the snowman have trunks and limbs of Burnt Umber, shade along the trunks with Burnt Umber. 'Needles' are Evergreen, shaded with Evergreen along both sides of the needles.

Step 3: The top section of the hat is shaded above the hatband with Deep Midnight Blue, and highlighted with Light Buttermilk along the top.

Step 4: The hatband is shaded along the bottom with Burnt Umber, highlighted along the top with Buttermilk, and lined at the top with Soft Black. The vine wrapping around the band is Burnt Umber, using the #18/0 liner. Float a highlight on the front of the brim with Buttermilk.

Birdhouses on hat:

Step 5: The mauve house is shaded with Rookwood Red, with Soft Black grain lines from the roof. The highlight in the heart hole and along the bottom of the house is Light Buttermilk.

Step 6: The tan house is shaded with Burnt Umber; highlight in the hole is Light Buttermilk. Add grain lines of Soft Black from the rooftop.

Step 7: The green house is shaded with Evergreen, with Soft Black grain lines from the roof. The highlight in the hole and along the bottom of the house is Light Buttermilk.

Step 8: The round base has small checks of French Grey Blue using the #1 flat. A

Step 9: The vines wrapping around the edge of the base are Burnt Umber tipped in Khaki Tan, and Buttermilk as needed-using the 18/0 liner. The leaves are double-loaded in Jade Green and Evergreen, using the #1 flat.

FINISHING DETAILS

Step 1: Spatter (flyspeck) over the candleholders with Burnt Umber and then Light Buttermilk.

Step 2: Erase any remaining graphite and varnish as desired. Enjoy!!

"Oh Snow Happy"

(Tin Bucket) (color photo - page 32)

"Doesn't this snowman look happy, playing in the meadow with his Christmas toy? This neat little tin bucket w/lid would be a nice addition to your Christmas collection. I think it would also make a great gift for the snowman lover in your family. Have fun and happy painting!"

Surface/Supplier:
Item # 1616212 -Green Tree Cutout Basket
Painter's Paradise
111 Parrish Lane
Wilmington, Delaware 19810
(302) 478-7619 -voice
(302) 478-9441 -fax
jodecart@aol.com -email
http://www.paintersparadise.com

Palette:
Deco Art Americana

Black Plum	Burnt Orange
Burnt Umber	Buttermilk
Camel	French Grey Blue
Jade Green	Khaki Tan
Light Buttermilk	Mauve
Mississippi Mud	Payne's Grey
Plantation Pine	Raw Sienna
Rookwood Red	Sable Brown
Soft Black	Uniform Blue

Misc. Supplies:
Deco Art Snow Tex

Brushes:
Loew/Cornell Golden Taklon
Series 7550 Glaze/Wash No. 3/4, 1/2
Series 7300 Shaders Nos. 4, 2, 1
Series 7050 Script Liners No.18/0
Series 7000 Rounds No. 3
Series DM Stipplers No. 1/4
Series Maxine Mops 3/4, 1/2

INSTRUCTIONS

Step 1: No preparation is necessary, just base coat the lid in Uniform Blue.

Step 2: Apply the pattern lightly and base coat as follows:

INITIAL BASECOATS

Snowman: Buttermilk
Stick Arms: Mississippi Mud
Gloves: Jade Green
Jacket: Mauve; Trim is Khaki Tan
Toy/Decoration-
Snowman: Buttermilk
Beads between snowmen: Camel;
And descending in order downward:
   Mauve; Jade Green; Camel; Mauve

SHADING AND DETAIL

❄ *Refer to inked dots on the pattern for shading placement, keep in mind that the denser the dots - the darker the shading should be.*

Snowman:

Step 1: Float the background next to the body (under arms, above arms walking outward) with French Grey Blue; this will give a soft "glow" to the scene.

Step 2: Shade him with Mississippi Mud and then float a soft side-load glaze of Uniform Blue down the Right side. Highlight with Light Buttermilk on the chin, belly and in a slip-slap manner in a few areas of the lower body. (Apply side-loaded paint in a circular manner, using a tapping motion.)

Step 3: Apply the pattern for the face and buttons. Paint the features in with Soft Black, the nose is Burnt Orange, and the buttons are Soft Black. The cheeks are dry-brushed on with Rookwood Red. Add a highlight in the eyes, cheeks and buttons with Light Buttermilk. Highlight the face, above the nose, with Light Buttermilk (walk it upwards). Shade under the nose/buttons with Mississippi Mud. Line the bottom of the nose with Burnt Umber.

Stick Arms:
Step 1: Shade and line with Burnt Umber, float the topside with Buttermilk.

Gloves:
Step 1: The plaid gloves are painted with the #1 flat and Plantation Pine; line between with Light Buttermilk; shade with Plantation Pine and drybrush the highlight with Light Buttermilk, in the open areas of the glove, away from the shading. Float a glaze (side-loaded) of Rookwood Red in a couple areas on the gloves. The strings are lined in Light Buttermilk.

Jacket:
Step 1: The jacket has stripes of Rookwood Red, use the #4 flat. Line between with Black Plum, using the 18/0 liner. Shade with Rookwood Red and deepen shading with Black Plum. Highlight with a drybrush of Mauve plus a touch of Light Buttermilk. Line/stitch and add hearts with Soft Black. The connecting string is Soft Black, over-stroked with Light Buttermilk.
Step 2: The lower section is shaded with Burnt Umber and highlighted with Buttermilk. The checks are Rookwood Red (#2 flat), dot between with Soft Black. The lettering is Soft Black, stitch at the top with Buttermilk.

Toy/Decoration:
Snowmen:
Step 1: Shade the snowmen with Mississippi Mud, highlight with Light Buttermilk down the Left side and side-load glaze a float of Uniform Blue down the Right side.
Step 2: Apply the pattern for the features (or freehand!) and put them in with Soft Black. The nose is Burnt Orange. The heart buttons are Soft Black. The wire arms are painted in with Light Buttermilk. Add a little color in the cheeks with Rookwood Red, by lightly moistening the cheek area and side loading a tiny float on the cheeks.
Step 3: The beads are all shaded with the following colors, down the lower right side:
Camel: Float with Raw Sienna
Mauve: Float with Rookwood Red
Jade Green: Float with Plantation Pine.
Step 4: Highlight the beads with an upper left float and dot, of Light Buttermilk.

Trees:
Step 1: Stroke the tree trunks on with Sable Brown; pull the stroke all the way up to the top of the tree.
Step 2: Side-load float the limbs on with Jade Green, using the 1/2" flat. Pull the strokes upwards (Jade Green faces down and the water side faces up). When placing the strokes (limbs) make them a bit uneven, it will look more natural than having them in perfect rows. Further brighten some of the branches, by going over them with a soft side-load of Light Buttermilk.
Step 3: Shade under the layers of branches with a side-load of Plantation Pine.
Step 4: Side-load Burnt Umber and softly tap color up through the center of the tree, right where the trunk is. Shade the trunk by pushing a side-load of Burnt Umber up under/into the limbs.

Snow:
Step 1: The snow is floated on first with Buttermilk, (build up fairly opaque under the snowman) then brighten further with floats of Light Buttermilk, right under/around the snowman.
Step 2: Add small touches of Snow Tex on the brightest -highest- parts of the snow.

FINISHING DETAILS
Step 1: Float around the perimeter of the lid with Payne's Grey.
Step 2: Spatter the scene with Light Buttermilk. Erase any remaining graphite, varnish as desired. Happy painting!

"No Humbugs Allowed"

"Oh Snow Happy"

 # "Oh Christmas Tree"

(Christmas Ornaments) (color photo - page 32)

"These three whimsical trees will be a unique addition to your ornament collection. I think it would be really neat to personalize them, just write the name or date in one of the light colored sections of the tree. Enjoy!"

Surface/Supplier:
"Bear with Us" Puffy Trees
Treasures of the Heart
119 S. Old Pacific Hwy.
Myrtle Creek, OR 97457
(541) 863-4466
treasuresoftheheart@hotmail.com

Palette:
Deco Art Americana

Black Plum	Burnt Orange
Burnt Umber	Deep Midnight Blue
Evergreen	Jade Green
Khaki Tan	Light Buttermilk
Mauve	Mississippi Mud
Rookwood Red	Soft Black

Brushes:
Loew/Cornell Golden Taklon
Series 7550 Glaze/Wash No. 1/2
Series 7050 Script Liners No. 18/0
Series 7000 Rounds No. 1
Series DM Stipplers No. 1/8"
Series Maxine Mops Nos. 1/2"

INSTRUCTIONS

❆ You might want to decide before painting how you will hang the trees, if you need to have holes drilled…you may want to do that before painting.

Step 1: Sand, seal and sand again. Apply the pattern to separate the sections:

All Trees: The 2nd and 4th sections are based in Jade Green.

Tree #1: The 1st, 3rd and 5th layers are based in Evergreen.

Tree #2: The 1st, 3rd and 5th layers are based in Deep Midnight Blue.

Tree #3: The top section is based in Rookwood Red, the middle section is based in Evergreen and the bottom section is based in Deep Midnight Blue.

SHADING AND DETAIL

❆ **Note:** All of the trees 2nd and 4th Jade Green sections, are painted in the same manner:

Step 1: Line/plaid with Evergreen, and then with Mauve. Shade with Evergreen.

Step 2: The vines are Mississippi Mud, pulled through Khaki Tan and Burnt Umber as needed to define.

Tree #1- Apply the pattern for the faces.

Step 1: All snowmen faces are based in Light Buttermilk. Float down the left sides with Mississippi Mud, and across the top with Deep Midnight Blue.

Step 2: Apply the pattern for the features and base them in Soft Black- except for the noses, which are Burnt Orange. Line the bottom of the noses with Soft Black. Highlight in the eyes and cheeks with Light Buttermilk.

Tree #2-Apply the pattern for the snowmen.

Step 1: Base the snowmen in Light Buttermilk. Shade under the snowmen rounds with Deep Midnight Blue and then float down the Left side with Burnt Umber.

Step 2: The stick arms are Mississippi Mud. The features are Soft Black- except for the tiny carrot noses, which are Burnt Orange.

Step 3: Side-load float snow behind/ around the bodies, with Light Buttermilk. With a liner brush, tap snow (Light Buttermilk) around the bodies, so that it looks like little snowballs. Add falling snow with the liner and Light Buttermilk, also.

(continued on page 30)

(continued from page 29)

Tree #3- Apply the pattern.

Step 1: The heart is based in Mauve, shade the bottom with Rookwood Red and highlight the top with Light Buttermilk. Shade around the heart with Black Plum. Add a dot above with Light Buttermilk.

Step 2: Pull the trunk down with Mississippi Mud tipped in Khaki Tan. Stroke the limbs on with Jade Green and then float beside the trunk (over the limbs) with Evergreen, to tone down the limbs. The dot on the top is Mauve.

Step 3: The background snow is floated on with Light Buttermilk. The house is based in Khaki Tan, shaded with Burnt Umber. The door and window are Soft Black. The roof is shaded on the back edge with Burnt Umber and across the top with Deep Midnight Blue. The snowman and snow are painted the same as in Tree #2.

FINISHING DETAILS

Step 1: Erase any remaining graphite and varnish as desired. Hang the ornaments by drilling a hole in the top or by screwing in an eye screw and hanging with ribbon.

"Oh Christmas Tree"

"Christmas Treasures"
(Square Box) (color photo - page 32)

"Gathered together on a snowy winter's eve, this fuzzy haired doll (whom I have named Flo, after my sweet friend)…and her snowman friend are patiently awaiting Christmas morn. This wonderful little box can be filled with special gifts or ornaments for your loved one."

Surface/Supplier:
Item #LSQD-18 Square Box
Valhalla Designs
343 Twin Pines Drive
Glendale, OR 97442
(541) 832-3260
http://www.ValhallaDesigns.com

Palette:
Deco Art Americana

Antique White	Black Plum
Burnt Umber	Buttermilk
Camel	Deep Midnight Blue
French Grey Blue	Gingerbread
Jade Green	Khaki Tan
Light Buttermilk	Mauve
Mississippi Mud	Payne's Grey
Plantation Pine	Raw Sienna
Rookwood Red	Slate Grey
Soft Black	

Brushes:
Loew/Cornell Golden Taklon
Series 7550 Wash/Glaze No. 1/2, 3/4
Series 7300 Shaders No. 8, 4, 1
Series 7050 Script Liners No. 18/0
Series 7000 Rounds No. 1
Series DM Stippler No. 1/2, 1/4
Series Maxine Mops No. 3/4, 1/2

Misc. Supplies:
3/4" Scotch Brand Magic Tape

INSTRUCTIONS
Step 1: Sand, seal and sand again.
Step 2: Basecoat the box top in Deep Midnight Blue, and the bottom in Plantation Pine.
Step 3: Apply pattern and basecoat as follows:

INITIAL BASECOATS
Snowman: Buttermilk
Scarf: French Grey Blue; Khaki Tan band (use #8 flat).
Pail: Slate Grey
Flag: Base in Antique White; Red stripes are Rookwood Red; Union is French Grey Blue
Flag Pole: Mississippi Mud
Tree: Base the trunk in Mississippi Mud
Tree Topper Birdhouse: Camel
Christmas Balls: Jade, Mauve, French Grey Blue
Fuzzy Haired Flo (doll): Face-hands-legs are Antique White
Flo's Dress: Jade Green; collar of Light Buttermilk.

SHADING AND DETAIL
Snowman:
Step 1: Shade with soft floats of Mississippi Mud and highlight with Light Buttermilk.
Step 2: Stitching and lettering are Mississippi Mud.
Step 3: The eyes-brows-lips are lined in with Soft Black.
Step 4: The nose is based n Gingerbread, float Rookwood Red on the bottom and add a soft float across the top with Light Buttermilk.
Step 5: Float Rookwood Red across the lip, and dry-brush the cheeks with Rookwood Red
Step 6: Highlights in the eyes and cheeks are Light Buttermilk.

Scarf:
Step 1: Shade with soft floats of Deep Midnight Blue and create the folds/pleats in the scarf. Deepen floats with Payne's Grey in the darkest areas. Highlight with a brush mix of French Grey Blue and Light Buttermilk, and then further highlights with Light Buttermilk.
Step 2: The Khaki Tan band along the bottom is dotted and shaded with Burnt Umber; highlighted with Light Buttermilk. The fringe is Mississippi Mud with Burnt Umber dots.

(continued on page 36)

(continued from page 35)

Pail:
Step 1: Float Soft Black down the sides and inside the front edge. Float Light Buttermilk down the center front, using a reverse float.

Step 2: Line with Soft Black along brim, bottom and handle use Slate Grey to highlight as needed.

Step 3: The hearts and leaves are Light Buttermilk, line and then float the bottom of the heart with Rookwood Red. The leaves are lined and floated with Plantation Pine. Add a Soft Black dot below leaves.

Flag:
Step 1: The Union is shaded with Deep Midnight Blue and highlighted with Light Buttermilk; the star is Light Buttermilk, float Mississippi Mud over the right side of the star.

Step 2: The red stripes are shaded with Black Plum. The white stripes are shaded with Burnt Umber. Highlight with Light Buttermilk across the outer edge. Add an Antique White outline around the flag, ending with a swirl.

Flag Pole:
Step 1: The pole is floated down the Right side with Burnt Umber; highlight the front edge with Antique White. The vines are stroked on by loading the 18/0 liner in Plantation Pine and pulling through Jade Green. The leaves are fully loaded in Jade and side-loaded in Plantation Pine, use the #4 flat.

Tree Top Birdhouse:
Step 1: Shade Raw Sienna and highlight with Buttermilk. The base and roof are Mississippi Mud, while wet tip in Buttermilk to highlight.

Step 2: The star is Camel; float Camel around the star for a glow. The post is Slate Grey. The holes are Soft Black.

Tree:
Step 1: The trunk is shaded with Burnt Umber.

Step 2: With the #8 flat double-loaded in Jade and Plantation Pine, and the Jade edge facing down...pull up and tap branches across the layers. *TIP: Leave the Deep Midnight Blue background showing as dark shadows between the layers.

Step 3: Load the 1/2" brush in Light Buttermilk and touch the front and center branches for brightest highlights.

Fuzzy Haired Flo (doll):
Step 1: Shade the face with Mississippi Mud, line/stitch with Mississippi Mud. Highlight with Light Buttermilk. The eyes/mouth are Soft Black and the nose is Mauve. Pre-wet the cheeks lightly with water, and then float a semi-circular float of Rookwood Red, add highlight dots of Light Buttermilk.

❋**Note:** Finish the Flo's dress and then come back and paint her hair:

Hair:
Step 1: The hair is inky Raw Sienna (18/0 liner), pull through inky Camel and build up most of the curls. Then pull the brush through inky Burnt Umber and add a few dark curls.

Step 2: Float next to the head with a brush mix of Camel and Raw Sienna. Then re-stroke the curls with Camel and then Light Buttermilk to further lighten, if desired.

Flo's Dress:
Step 1: Float Plantation Pine to shade the doll's dress, and highlight with Light Buttermilk. The stripes are Mauve (#4 flat) with a Plantation Pine stripe. Float the mauve stripes with Rookwood Red, and highlight with Light Buttermilk.

Step 2: The collar is floated with Mississippi Mud and highlighted with Light Buttermilk. Add lace with Light Buttermilk, and the heart with Rookwood Red.

Step 3: The doll's dolly's body is based in Antique White and is shaded with Mississippi Mud and the dress is Buttermilk, shaded with Mississippi Mud and lined with Burnt Umber. The buttons, hair and features are Soft Black.

Step 4: The candy cane is based in with Light Buttermilk, using the #1 flat. Add the red stripes with Rookwood Red, using the #4 flat. Float Payne's Grey down the backside and under the hook of the cane.

Christmas Balls:
Step 1: Green ball has detail lines of Rookwood Red; add tiny strokes with the #1 round and Plantation Pine. Float Plantation Pine across the bottom, and highlight with Light Buttermilk across the top.

Step 2: Blue ball has detail lines of Deep Midnight Blue; dots of Deep Midnight Blue and Light Buttermilk; and shaded with Deep Midnight Blue across the bottom. Highlight across the top with Light Buttermilk.

Step 3: Red ball has zigzag detail of Rookwood Red and Light Buttermilk. Float Rookwood Red across the bottom, deepen with Black Plum and highlight with Light Buttermilk on the top.

Step 4: The caps on the balls are based in Camel and overstroked on the Left side with Raw Sienna. The hangers on the balls are stroked on with Buttermilk.

Snow:

Step 1: With the 3/4" brush side-loaded in Light Buttermilk, begin softly floating the snow on, building the layers up. Move to the 1/2" brush and continue building up the snow with smaller mounds of snow.

TIPS

- Wash the brush out and re-load as needed to keep the water edge clean.
- Keep a little on the end/edge of the brush when building the depth, next to the objects (in other words-keep a glob on the brush!)
- Make dabby, floating "C" shapes to create the small mounds.
- Use water edge of brush to smooth out the bottoms of the floats that may pick up the color.
- Use a mop brush to soften and pull the color.

(continued on page 38)

(continued from page 37)

Sides of the Box:

Step 1: Using the 3/4" tape, tape off the edge of the box, and paint the sections with Jade Green. Remove the tape and add a stripe down the center of each green stripe with the #8 flat and Deep Midnight Blue. Shade the top and bottoms of the stripes with Payne's Grey. Add Buttermilk dots.

FINISHING DETAILS

Step 1: Float Payne's Grey around the objects of the scene, and the outer edges of the box.

Step 2: Spatter with Light Buttermilk over the box. Erase any remaining graphite and varnish as desired. Enjoy!

"Sweet Ginger Angel"

(Wobbly Angel) (color photo - page 31)

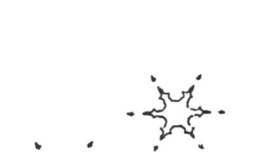

"This fun, wobbly Gingerbread angel will make you smile as she shows off her Snow folk family. She sits on a base that has a strong spring so that she wobbles when you touch her. Too fun!"

Surface/Supplier:
Provo Craft - Wobbly Angel
Treasures of the Heart
119 S. Old Pacific Hwy.
Myrtle Creek, OR 97457
(541) 863-4466
treasuresoftheheart@hotmail.com

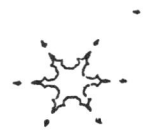

Palette:
Deco Art Americana

Antique White	Burnt Orange
Burnt Umber	Buttermilk
Deep Midnight Blue	Khaki Tan
Mauve	Mississippi Mud
Payne's Grey	Plantation Pine
Rookwood Red	Sable Brown
Soft Black	

Brushes:
Loew/Cornell Golden Taklon
Series 7550 Glaze/Wash No. 1/2
Series 7300 Shaders Nos. 4, 2
Series 7050 Script Liners No. 18/0
Series 7000 Rounds No. 3
Series DM Stipplers No. 3/8, 1/8
Series Maxine Mops Nos. 3/4, 1/2

INSTRUCTIONS

Step 1: Sand, seal and sand again. Wrap the colors/design around the angel, if desired. Base as follows:

INITIAL BASECOATS

Face/hands/base: Base in Sable Brown
Shirt: Khaki Tan; **Cuffs:** Mauve
Dress: Deep Midnight Blue
Top band on hem: Mauve
Bottom band on hem: Antique White
Tin Wings: Khaki Tan

SHADING AND DETAIL

Face/hands/base:

Step 1: Apply frosting with Buttermilk. Dot between with Buttermilk.

Step 2: Shade under/around the frosting with Burnt Umber. Drybrush with Buttermilk here and there in the open areas.

Step 3: Apply the pattern for the features and fill them in with Soft Black, -except for the nose, which is based in Rookwood Red. Drybrush the cheeks on with Rookwood Red, add highlights in the eyes, nose and cheeks with Buttermilk. Float Rookwood Red on the lower lip.

Step 4: Check the bottom edge of the wobbly base with the #2 flat and Burnt Umber.

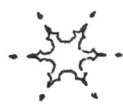

Shirt:

Step 1: Stripe with Buttermilk and then with Rookwood Red., shade with Burnt Umber. Add stitches above the cuffs with Buttermilk. Drybrush down the center of the sleeves with Buttermilk.

Step 2: The necklace is dots of Buttermilk, with a Rookwood Red heart.

Step 3: The cuffs have checks of Rookwood Red (#4 flat) with a stripe of Buttermilk through the center.

Dress:

Step 1: Apply the pattern for the snowmen and base them in Buttermilk.

Step 2: Shade the dress, around the snowmen with Payne's Grey. Shade around the doll's arms and at the shoulders with Payne's Grey. Dot the falling snow on with Buttermilk and the stylus. Line and stitch around the opening with Buttermilk.

Step 3: The snow people are shaded with Mississippi Mud, under the chins and down the Left side. Float down the Right side with Deep Midnight Blue.

Step 4: The features are Soft Black, except for the noses, which are Burnt Orange. Drybrush the cheeks on with Rookwood Red, using the small DM Stippler. Stitches are Soft Black. The twig arms are Burnt Umber tipped in Antique White. The twig heart is Burnt Umber, shaded with Burnt Umber. The buttons down the (L-R) snowmen are Rookwood Red on snowmen 1,3,5 and Deep Midnight Blue down snowman 2, and Plantation Pine on snowman 4.

Top band on hem:

Step 1: Stripe with Rookwood Red and the #4 flat. Shade along the bottom with Rookwood Red, and highlight the top edge with Buttermilk.

Bottom band on hem:

Step 1: Shade the bottom with Mississippi Mud and highlight the top with Buttermilk. Stitch along the bottom edge with Buttermilk.

Step 2: Stroke on the leaf pattern with Plantation Pine and the #3 round. The dot between is Rookwood Red.

Tin Wings:

Step 1: Float the outer edge of the wings with Burnt Umber, drybrush through the center with Buttermilk.

Step 2: The vines around the edges are Burnt Umber, using the 18/0 liner.

FINISHING DETAILS

Step 1: Erase any remaining graphite and varnish as desired. Enjoy!

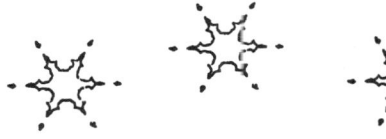

"Homespun Christmas"

(Box) (color photo - page 31)

"Another wonderful little box to hold special ornaments or trinkets at Christmastime. If you haven't noticed, I love the color blue (in most any shade), but this piece would also look nice painted with a Khaki Tan background, or even Rookwood Red. Experiment and have fun!"

Surface/Supplier:
Item # SSQD-14 Sm. Square Divided Box
Valhalla Designs
343 Twin Pines Drive
Glendale, OR 97442
(541) 832-3260
http://www.ValhallaDesigns.com

Palette:
Deco Art Americana

Antique White
Buttermilk
Deep Midnight Blue
Gingerbread
Khaki Tan
Mauve
Mississippi Mud
Plantation Pine
Rookwood Red
Soft Black
Burnt Umber
Camel
French Grey Blue
Jade Green
Light Buttermilk
Mink Tan
Payne's Grey
Raw Sienna
Sable Brown

Brushes:
Loew/Cornell Golden Taklon
Series 7550 Glaze/Wash No. 3/4, 1/2
Series 7300 Shaders No. 4, 2
Series 7050 Script Liners No. 18.0
Series 7000 Rounds No. 3, 1
Series DM Stipplers No. 3/8
Series Maxine Mops No. 3/4,
Misc. Supplies:
1/2" Scotch Brand Magic Tape
Sea Sponge
Deco Art Snow Tex (optional)

INSTRUCTIONS

Step 1: Sand, seal and sand again. Base the lid in Deep Midnight Blue and the bottom in French Grey Blue.

Step 2: Using the 1/2" tape, tape off every other stripe. Dampen the sea sponge in water and tip into French Grey Blue, swirl blend on palette and then sponge the taped off edge of the box. *Instructions for the detail on the side of the box, is given under the Finishing Details.

Step 3: Apply pattern lightly and basecoat as follows.

INITIAL BASECOATS

Birdhouse: French Grey Blue
Chimney: Mauve
Roof: Khaki Tan
Star Hole: Camel
Gingerbread Doll-
Face/Arms/Legs: Sable Brown
Dress: Khaki Tan; Lace Trim is Antique White.
Apron: Mauve; Bodice and Hem are Antique White.
Snowman: Buttermilk
Buttons: Jade Green and Mauve.

SHADING AND DETAIL

Birdhouse:

Step 1: Shade and add grain lines with Deep Midnight Blue. With Deep Midnight Blue float around the star hole, leaving an 1/8" margin. Drybrush in the open areas of the house, with Light Buttermilk.

Step 2: For the wreath, pull strokes of Khaki Tan around the star hole. Add lighter strokes of Antique White, and then shade over the wreath with Burnt Umber.

Step 3: The perch is Soft Black, highlight with Light Buttermilk on the top.

Chimney:

Step 1: Check the chimney, using the #4 flat and

washy Rookwood Red. Highlight with Buttermilk on the Right side and shade with Rookwood Red.

Step 2: The smoke coming from the chimney is Buttermilk, side-load float with the 1/2" brush.

Roof:

Step 1: Shade the top of the Left side and the bottom of the Right side with Burnt Umber. Highlight with Buttermilk on the lower Left side and on the upper Right side.

Star Hole:

Step 1: Shade inside the hole with Raw Sienna and deepen with Burnt Umber. The screening is Soft Black, using the 18/0 liner.

Step 2: Add a line around the hole with Light Buttermilk, float next to this line with Light Buttermilk.

Gingerbread Doll-
Face/Arms/Legs:

Step 1: The frosting is Antique White. Shade the face/arms/legs/frosting with Burnt Umber. Highlight the face/arms/legs with Mink Tan, further highlight with Buttermilk. The frosting is highlight with Light Buttermilk. Stitch with Mississippi Mud.

Step 2: The features are Soft Black; the nose (optional) is Rookwood Red. Drybrush the cheeks with Rookwood Red, and float the lip with Rookwood Red. Highlight in the eyes/cheeks with Light Buttermilk

Dress:

Step 1: Dot and highlight the dress with Buttermilk. Shade with Mississippi Mud and deepen shading with Burnt Umber.

Step 2: The hem ruffle is shaded and lined with Mississippi Mud; deepen shading with Burnt Umber and highlight with Light Buttermilk. The lace trim edging is Light Buttermilk; use the 18/0 liner.

Apron:

Step 1: Stripe the apron with Rookwood Red and the #2 flat. Shade with Rookwood Red and highlight with Buttermilk.

Step 2: The bodice and lower band is shaded with Mississippi Mud, and highlighted with Light Buttermilk. Add a line with Light Buttermilk, using the 18/0 liner. Stitch with Mississippi Mud; add detail leaves of Plantation Pine with the #1 round and Rookwood Red dots.

Snowman:

Step 1: Shade with Mississippi Mud, and highlight with Light Buttermilk.

Step 2: The features are Soft Black; nose is Gingerbread; cheeks are dry-brushed on with Rookwood Red; lip is glazed with Rookwood Red. A highlight in the cheeks/eyes is Light Buttermilk. Add a halo with Buttermilk.

Step 3: The Mauve button is shaded with Rookwood Red, highlighted with Buttermilk. Line the bottom and add holes with Soft Black. The thread is Light Buttermilk.

Step 4: The Jade Green button is shaded with Plantation Pine, highlighted with Buttermilk. Line the bottom and add holes with Soft Black. The thread is Light Buttermilk.

Step 5: The vines around the buttons are Burnt Umber using the 18/0 liner. Shade softly around the vines with Burnt Umber.

Wings:

Step 1: Pull branches out first by loading the #18/0 liner in Mississippi Mud and tipping in Khaki Tan.

Step 2: The needles are stroked on with Jade Green tipped in Plantation Pine, further highlight with strokes of Jade Green only. Shade over them with Plantation Pine.

Step 3: The berries are Mauve Rookwood Red and highlighted with Light Buttermilk. Weave a few vines through the branches with Mississippi Mud, Khaki Tan and Burnt Umber.

Snow:

Step 1: Float snow under the scene with Light Buttermilk, using the 1/2" flat.

Step 2: Add Snowtex on the highest parts of the snow mounds, if desired.

(continued on page 42)

(continued from page 41)

FINISHING DETAILS

Step 1: Float Payne's Grey around the objects and the edges of the box.

Step 2: Spatter over the box with Light Buttermilk.

Step 3: The detail on the side of the box are strokes using the #1 round loaded in Plantation Pine, tipped in Jade Green. The berries are Mauve. Float the bottom of the side with Payne's Grey and the top with Light Buttermilk.

Step 4: Erase any remaining graphite and varnish as desired. Enjoy!

"Homespun Christmas"

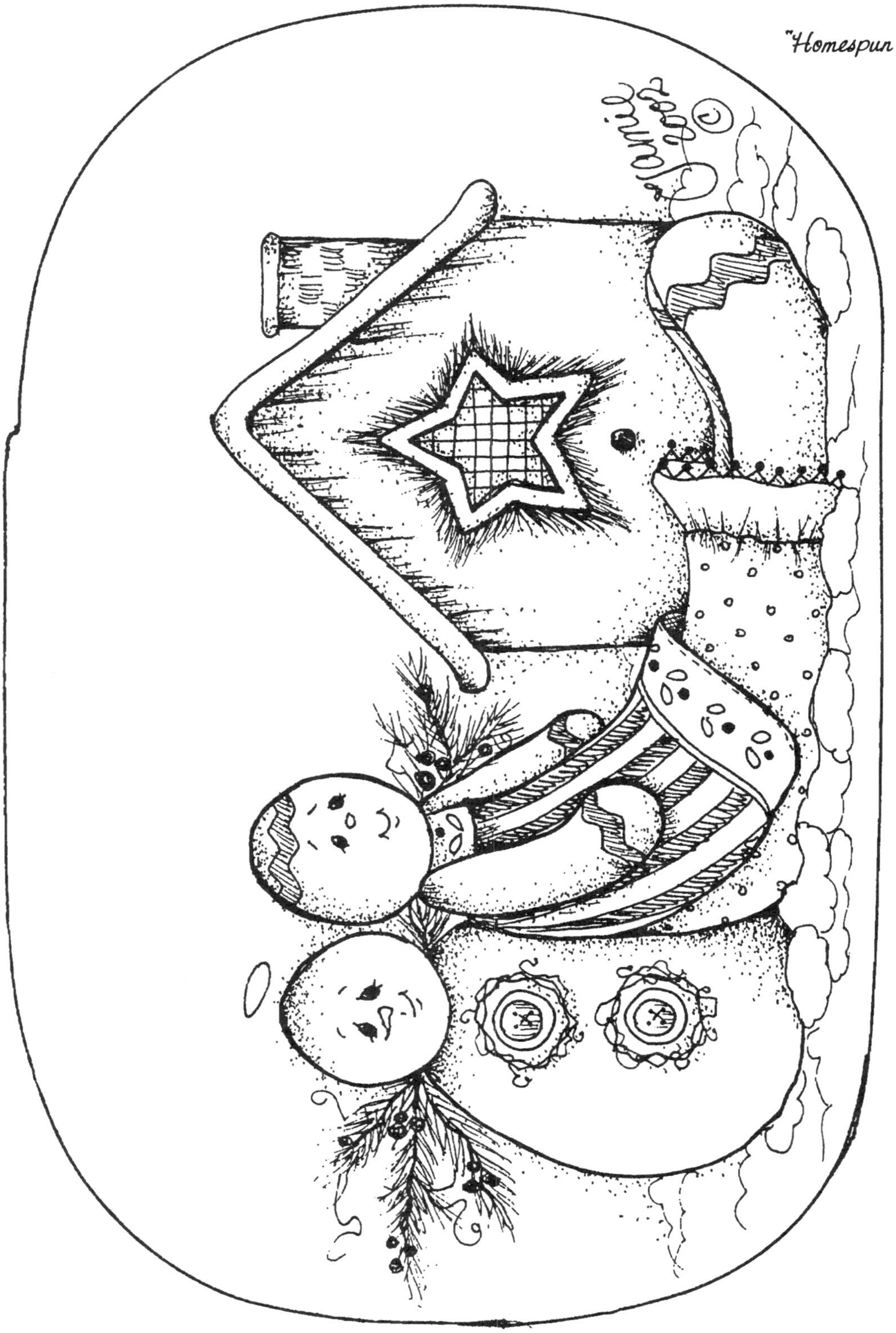

"Gingerbread Grins"

(Mini Sled Ornaments) (color photo - page 31)

"These mischievous gingerbread kids will look cute perched on your tree, you can personalize them instead of using the names on the banners. Enjoy!"

Surface/Supplier:
Mini Sleds set/3
Treasures of the Heart
119 S. Old Pacific Hwy.
Myrtle Creek, OR 97457
(541) 863-4466
treasuresoftheheart@hotmail.com

Palette:
Deco Art Americana

Antique Maroon	Burnt Umber
Buttermilk	Camel
French Grey Blue	Jade Green
Light Buttermilk	Mauve
Mink Tan	Mississippi Mud
Payne's Grey	Plantation Pine
Raw Sienna	Rookwood Red
Sable Brown	Soft Black
Uniform Blue	

Brushes:
Loew/Cornell Golden Taklon
Series 7550 Glaze/Wash No. 3/4, 1/2
Series 7300 Shaders Nos. 6, 4
Series 7050 Script Liners No. 18/0
Series DM Stipplers No. 3/8, 1/8
Series Maxine Mops 3/4, 1/2

INSTRUCTIONS
Step 1: Sand, seal and sand again. Basecoat the banners in Buttermilk; the sleds in Uniform Blue; the runners in Sable Brown.
Step 2: Apply pattern and basecoat as follows:

INITIAL BASECOATS
All Gingerbread: Sable Brown
Star: Buttermilk
Heart: Mauve
Moon: Camel

SHADING AND DETAIL
All Sleds:
Step 1: Shade around the perimeter of the sled (top) with Payne's Grey. Add small Mink Tan checks around the edges, and with Buttermilk add stitching on the checks.
Step 2: Float around the objects (gingerbread and shapes) with French Grey Blue, to give a soft glow to the piece.

All Runners:
Step 1: Float around all edges with Burnt Umber. Drybrush a highlight in the open areas of the runners with Mink Tan.

All Banners:
Step 1: Float Burnt Umber around the edges. The lettering is Soft Black, using the 18/0 liner.
Step 2: The leaf detail is Plantation Pine, using the #4 flat. The dots are Rookwood Red.

All Gingerbread:
Step 1: The icing is Buttermilk, using the 18/0 liner.
Step 2: Shade Burnt Umber and highlight with Mink Tan.
Step 3: The features are Soft Black; the nose is Rookwood Red; the cheeks are dry-brushed on with Rookwood Red. The buttons are Buttermilk.

Star:
Step 1: Stripe with French Grey Blue using the #6 flat. Line down the stripe with Uniform Blue, and add a line between with Mauve.
Step 2: Shade with Mississippi Mud and stitch with Burnt Umber. Drybrush in the center with Light Buttermilk.

(continued on page 44)

(continued from page 43)

"Gingerbread Grins"

Heart:
Step 1: Check with Antique Maroon, using the #6 flat. Shade with Antique Maroon, and drybrush a highlight in the center, with a brush mix of Mauve plus a touch of Buttermilk.
Step 2: Stitch with Soft Black.

Moon:
Step 1: Line and shade with Raw Sienna and highlight with Buttermilk.
Step 2: Stitch with Soft Black.

Vines and Leaves:
Step 1: The vines (18/0 liner) and leaves (#4 flat) are Jade Green.

FINISHING DETAILS
Step 1: Erase any remaining graphite and varnish as desired. Enjoy!

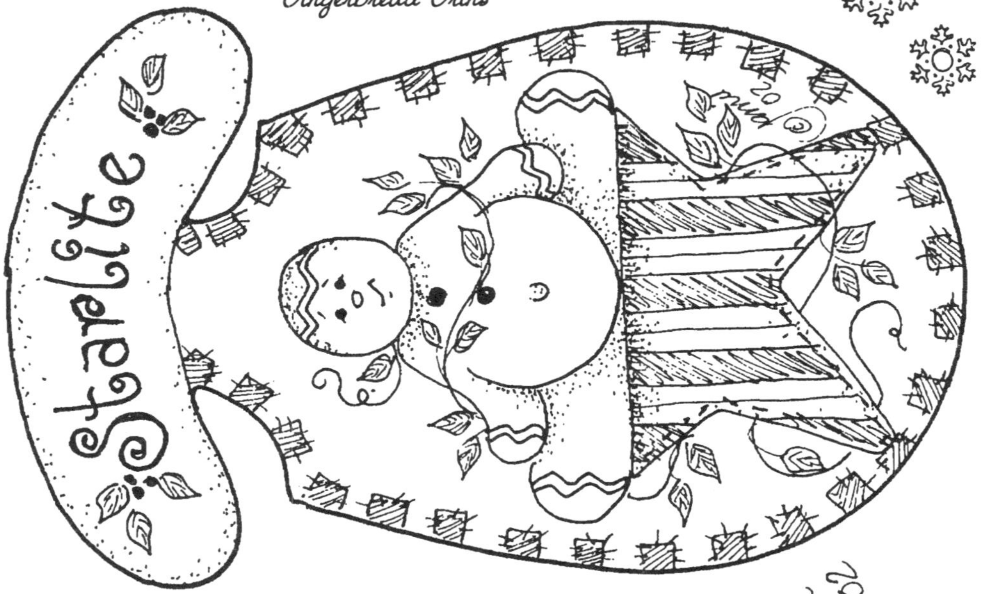

"Midnight Twinkles"

(Suds Dipper Pot) (color photo - page 33)

"This delightful bucket would be a wonderful candle or potpourri holder. I did not basecoat the background, but left it as it was...a nice chocolate brown/black. If you prefer you can basecoat the background in a dark blue, just experiment and have fun!"

Surface/Supplier:
Item # 811091 -Suds Dipper
Painters Paradise
111 Parrish Lane
Wilmington, Delaware 19810
(302) 478-7619 - Voice
(302) 478-9441 - Fax
jodecart@aol.com - email
http://www.paintersparadise.com

Palette:
Deco Art Americana

Burnt Orange	Burnt Umber
Buttermilk	Deep Midnight Blue
Jade Green	Light Buttermilk
Mauve	Mississippi Mud
Plantation Pine	Rookwood Red
Sable Brown	Soft Black

Misc. Supplies:
Deco Art Multi-Purpose Sealer

Brushes:
Loew/Cornell Golden Taklon
Series 7300 Shaders No. 6
Series 7550 Glaze/Wash No. 3/4, 1/2
Series 7050 No.18/0
Series 7000 Round No. 3
Series DM Stippler No. 1/4, 1/8
Series Maxine Mops No. 1/2, 3/4

INSTRUCTIONS

Note: I repeat...the background is not basecoated, but is left the color it came. If you like, you can base-coat it in a dark blue, green or burgundy would look nice.

Step 1: Brush the bucket (the outside) with the Multi-Purpose Sealer. This will prepare the surface, so that the paint will not bead up. It goes on milky, but will dry clear...no fear!

Step 2: The first thing I did was to float the snow on the background...if you like you can apply the pattern, or just freehand it Side-load the large 3/4" flat in Buttermilk and softly start floating on the snow, layering the color and building the brightness up gradually.

Step 3: We will paint the snowman and then build up the brightness of the snow with Light Buttermilk. Apply the pattern for the snow folk or freehand them on. The snowmen were stippled on with the 1/4" stippler and Buttermilk. Lightly moisten the stippler with water and then tap into Buttermilk, swirl on the palette to blend and then lightly start stippling in the shapes of the snowmen. I didn't fill them in so that they were opaque, but left them semi-transparent so that the background color still showed slightly.

Step 4: With a side-load of Buttermilk, using the 1/2" flat, float the bottoms of the top two rounds (chin and the belly) with Buttermilk...to shape them up a bit.

Step 5: With Mississippi Mud and the 1/2" flat, shade under the chin and the belly rounds.

Step 6: Using Deep Midnight Blue, float down the Right sides of the snowmen (on all three rounds).

Step 7: With a chunky side-load (leaving a little more paint on the edge) of Light Buttermilk, float down the Left side for the bright highlight.

Step 8: The features/buttons are Soft Black. The noses are Burnt Orange tipped in Burnt Umber. The cheeks are dry-brushed on with Rookwood Red. The twig arms are Sable Brown tipped in Buttermilk.

(continued on page 46)

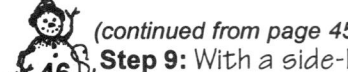

(continued from page 45)

Step 9: With a side-load of Light Buttermilk, come in now and float the snow on brighter around the snowmen, layer your color softly.

Vines and Leaves:

Step 1: Load the 18/0 liner in inky Sable Brown and pull through inky Buttermilk and/or Burnt Umber. The leaves are loaded fully in Jade and side-loaded in Plantation Pine, using the #6 flat.

The berries are Rookwood Red and Mauve, using the small end of a paintbrush.

FINISHING DETAILS

Step 1: Spatter with Light Buttermilk, using an old toothbrush or your favorite method.

Step 2: Varnish as desired...enjoy!

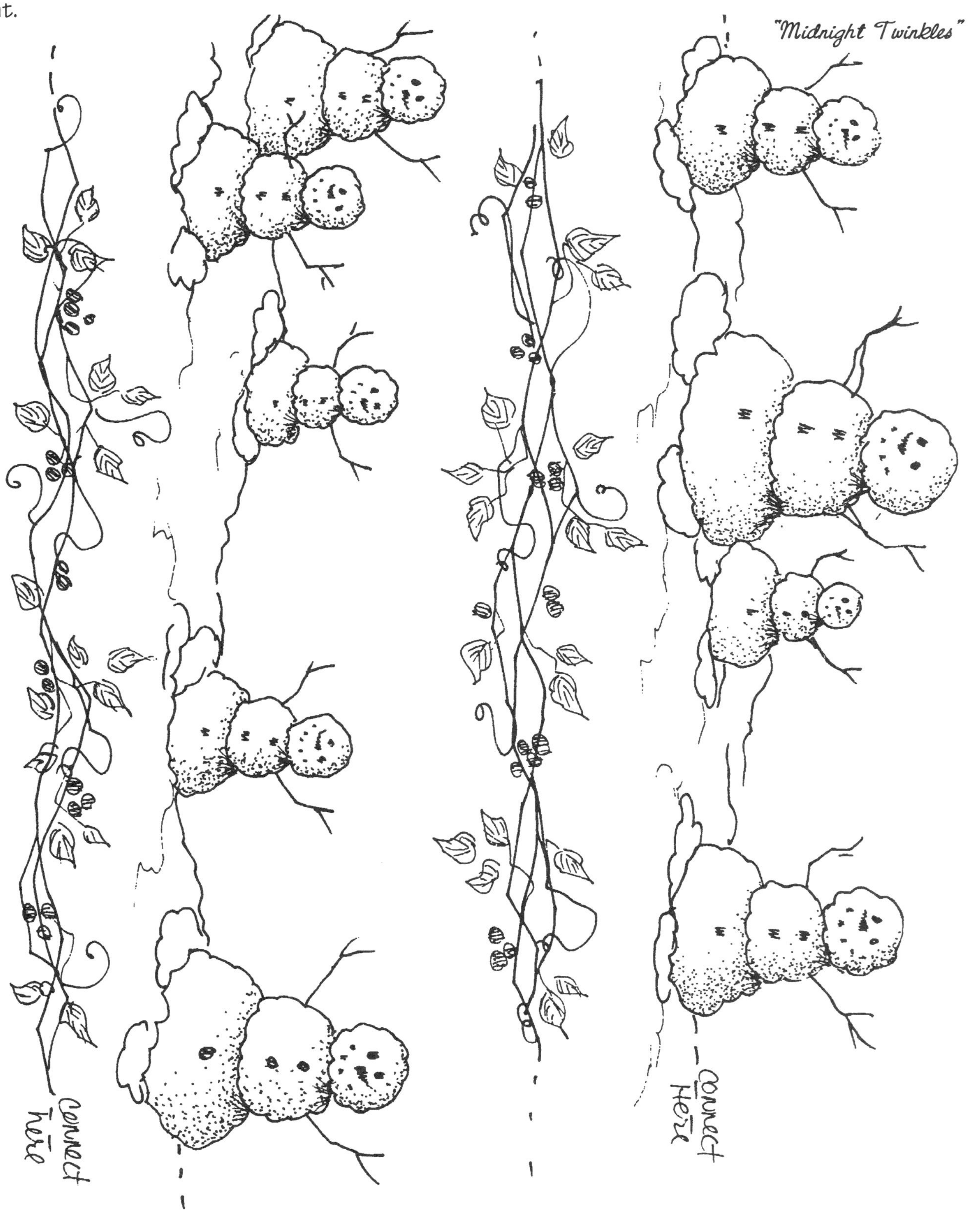

"Midnight Twinkles"

"Tiny Treasures"

(Framed Plaque) (color photo - page 33)

"This collection of merry Christmas characters will surely brighten up your holiday season. Feel free to change the frame color; I thought Rookwood Red would look nice also. A design for the reverse side of this insert panel will be included in Vines 7. Have fun painting!"

Surface/Supplier:
Rectangle Plaque w/insert
Item #: RP-41
Valhalla Designs
343 Twin Pines Drive
Glendale, OR 97442
(541) 832-3260
http://www.ValhallaDesigns.com

Palette:
Deco Art Americana

Antique Maroon	Antique White
Black Plum	Burnt Sienna
Burnt Umber	Buttermilk
Camel	Crimson Tide
Deep Midnight Blue	Eggshell
French Grey Blue	Gingerbread
Jade Green	Khaki Tan
Light Buttermilk	Mauve
Midnight Green	Mississippi Mud
Neutral Grey	Payne's Grey
Plantation Pine	Raw Sienna
Rookwood Red	Sable Brown
Slate Grey	Soft Black

Brushes:

Loew/Cornell Golden Taklon
Series 7550 Glaze/Wash No. 3/4, 1/2
Series 7300 Shaders No. 6, 4, 2, 1
Series 7000 Rounds No. 00,
Series 7050 Script Liner No. 18/0
Series DM Stipplers No. 1/2, 1/4, 1/8
Series Maxine's Mops No. 3/4, 1/2

INSTRUCTIONS
Step 1: Sand, seal and sand again. Base the frame in Deep Midnight Blue and the insert in Khaki Tan.
Step 2: Apply the pattern and basecoat as follows:

Initial Basecoats:
Snowman: Buttermilk
Bear: Face-hands-feet are Sable Brown; suit is Rookwood Red, trim is painted later.
Duck: Base body in Camel; beak in Gingerbread; wheels are Antique White.
Mouse: Slate Grey

Birdhouses:
Small - French Grey Blue; roof is Soft Black.
Medium - Jade Green; roof is Soft Black; ribbon/bow is Eggshell.
Large - Mauve; roof is Soft Black.
Birdhouse holes are Soft Black.
Tree: Heart tree topper is based in Camel.

SHADING AND DETAIL
Float around the objects in the scene softly with Burnt Umber.

Tree:
Step 1: The trunk/limbs are Burnt Umber, tipped into Mississippi Mud and stroked on. Shade with Soft Black. Float with Plantation Pine around the trunk and limbs.
Step 2: The dark green needles are Plantation Pine, stroked on with the #00 round. The fine needles between the large ones are first Plantation Pine and then over-stroked with Jade Green, using the 18/0 liner.
Step 3: The red balls on the tree are Crimson Tide, float around them with Crimson Tide and add a highlight with Light Buttermilk.
Step 4: The heart on the top is floated on the bottom with Raw Sienna, highlighted on the top with Light Buttermilk. Float around the heart with Raw Sienna.

(continued on page 48)

(continued from page 47)

Snowman:

Step 1: Shade the snowman softly with Mississippi Mud, deepen softly with Burnt Umber down the Right side, behind the bear. Glaze (soft side-load) French Grey Blue in several areas over the snowman. Such as: top of head; under neck; lower Left side; lower Right side; around hearts (after painting them!).

Step 2: Highlight with Light Buttermilk on chin and down the Left side.

Step 3: Apply pattern for features and hearts, fill in the eyes, mouth, brows and hearts with Soft Black. The nose is Rookwood Red, as are the dots above the hearts. Dry-brush the cheeks with Rookwood Red. Add highlights in the eyes, nose and cheeks with Light Buttermilk. The green stroke leaves are Plantation Pine, using the #6 flat.

Step 4: The stitching is Soft Black; the halo is Soft Black with a stroke of Light Buttermilk through the center.

Step 5: The 'wrought iron' wings are Soft Black (18/0 liner), add highlights of Slate Grey and further highlights of Light Buttermilk (in brightest areas). Float Soft Black here and there around the wings to soften and emphasize scrollwork.

Bear:

Step 1: The bear is shaded with Burnt Umber and highlighted with Antique White. The features are Soft Black; the cheeks are dry-brushed on with Rookwood Red. Highlight in the eyes and nose with Light Buttermilk.

Step 2: Shade the suit with Black Plum, and highlight with Crimson Tide. The buttons are Soft Black, highlighted with Buttermilk.

Step 3: The fur trim is stippled on with Slate Grey and Light Buttermilk, using the 1/8" stippler. Re-load your brush and adjust the color as needed.

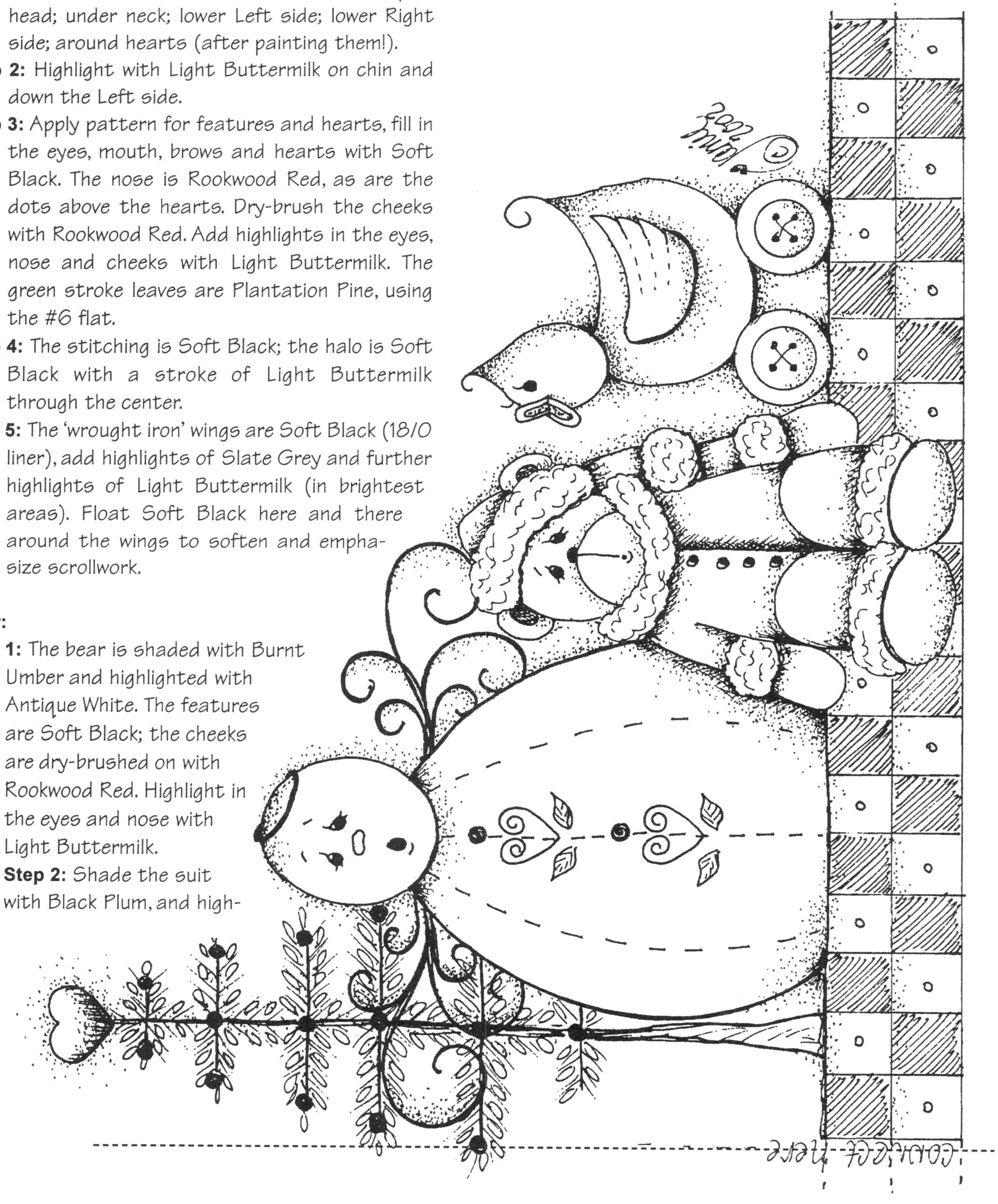

Duck:

Step 1: Shade with Raw Sienna and highlight with Buttermilk. Line/stitch with Raw Sienna on the wings, head, and tail.

Step 2: The beak is shaded with Burnt Sienna, line through the center with Soft Black. The eyes are Soft Black and the cheeks are dry-brushed on with Rookwood Red. Highlight in the eyes and cheek with Light Buttermilk.

Step 3: The wheels are shaded with Burnt Umber and highlighted with Light Buttermilk. The dots are Soft Black and the thread is Rookwood Red.

Mouse:

Step 1: The mouse is shaded with Neutral Grey, deepened with Soft Black. Highlight with Light Buttermilk. The features are lined in with Soft Black. Cheeks are dry-brushed on with Rookwood Red. Highlight in the eyes and nose with Light Buttermilk.

Step 2: Float in the ears with Mauve; add hair in ears, on head and whiskers with Light Buttermilk.

Birdhouses:
Small:
Step 1: Apply pattern for candles and base in Antique White, the drips in Buttermilk and the flame in Camel. Shade the house with Deep Midnight Blue under the roof, along the bottom and behind the candles. Deepen shading with Payne's Grey. Add grain lines with Soft Black. Highlight in the star hole with Light Buttermilk. The twig is Soft Black, highlighted with Light Buttermilk.

Step 2: Dry-brush in the open areas of the house with Light Buttermilk. The checks along the roof are Light Buttermilk, using the #2 flat.

Step 3: The candles are shaded with Mississippi Mud; deepen with Burnt Umber under the drips, and between the candles (on the recessed candle). Highlight with Light Buttermilk. The drips are shaded with Mississippi Mud, and highlighted with Light Buttermilk. The flames are shaded with Raw Sienna. The leaves are stroked on with the #4 flat, double-loaded in Plantation Pine and Jade Green. The vines are Plantation Pine and Jade Green. The berries are Crimson Tide.

Medium:

Step 1: Dot the house with Plantation Pine, and then shade the house and bow with Plantation Pine, deepen the shading on house and bow with Midnight Green. Dry-brush Light

(continued on page 50)

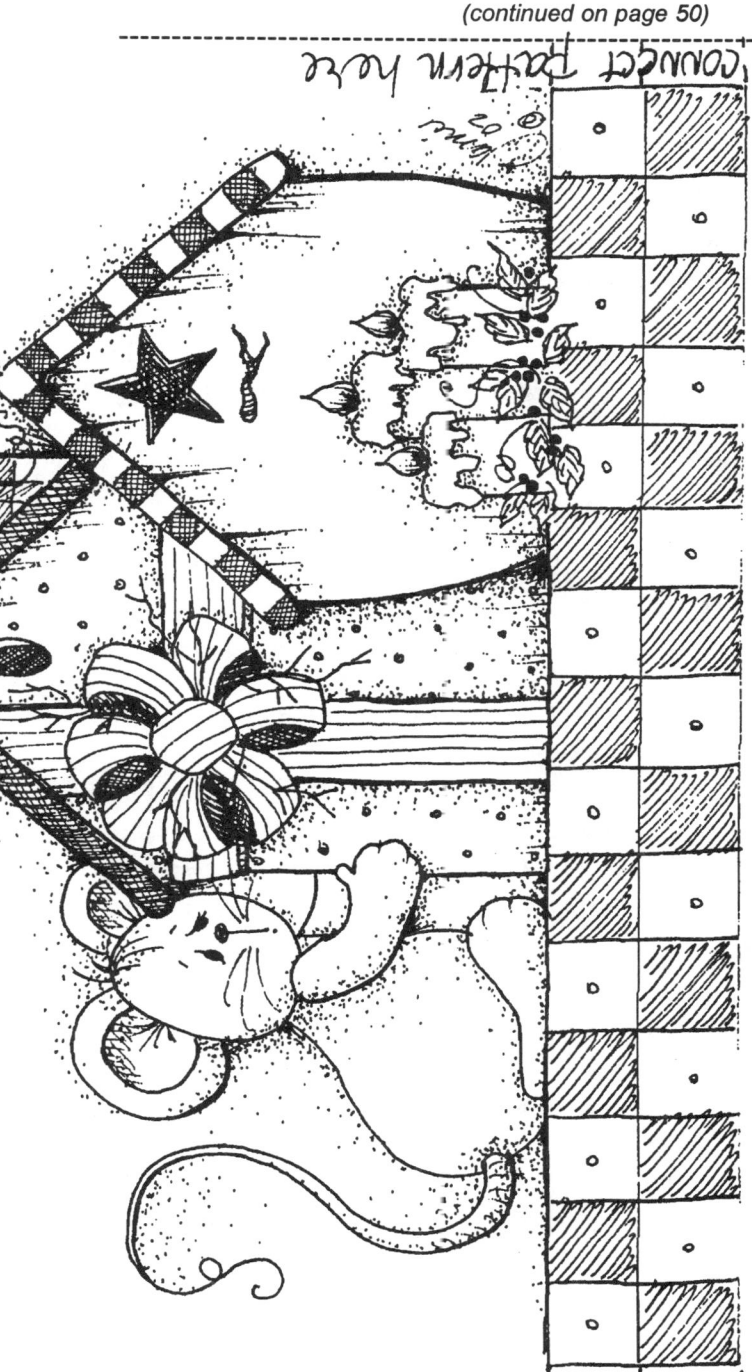

(continued from page 49)

Buttermilk in the open areas of the house, and highlight float with Light Buttermilk on the bow. After shading is complete, line the bow with Light Buttermilk and then softly re-float with Plantation Pine.

Step 2: Pull twig branches out of the bow with Burnt Umber. Highlight with Light Buttermilk in the hole. Highlight the roof with Light Buttermilk.

Large:

Step 1: Stripe the house with the #1 flat and Antique Maroon. Shade the house with Antique Maroon. Highlight in the holes and on the roof, with Light Buttermilk.

Step 2: The vines are Plantation Pine and Jade Green. The leaves are Midnight Green, using the #4 flat. The berries are Light Buttermilk, using the stylus.

Checks:

Step 1: Using the 1/2" brush and washy Deep Midnight Blue, add the checkerboard under the objects. Shade the tan checks with Burnt Umber and highlight with Buttermilk. Dots are Rookwood Red. Shade the top of the blue checks with Payne's Grey.

Frame:

Step 1: The twig star is Khaki Tan, using the 18/0 liner. Shade over the twig star with Burnt Umber. Base inside the star cutout with Khaki Tan, (Rookwood Red might look nice also). Sand the edges of the frame if desired.

FINISHING DETAILS

Step 1: Dry-brush in the open areas of the insert with Buttermilk, using the 1/2" stippler.

Step 2: Spatter over the insert with Buttermilk, using an old toothbrush or your favorite method.

Step 3: Re-shade around the objects if desired with Burnt Umber.

Step 4: Erase any remaining graphite and varnish as desired. Enjoy!!

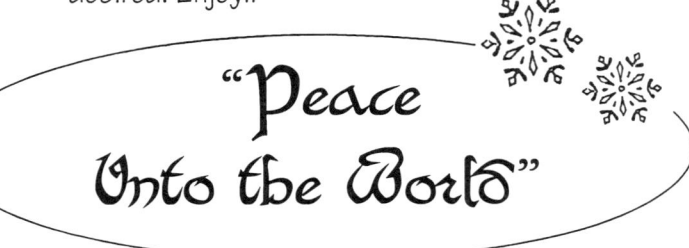

"Snowflake Tin"

(Tin Bowl) (color photo - inside back cover)

"I loved this little tin bowl with its snowflake cutouts and paintable lid. "Painter's Paradise" has some wonderful surfaces that I think would make unique and creative gifts for Christmas, or just to treat yourself anytime! This little container could hold potpourri or you could give it as a gift with a little trinket inside. Enjoy!"

Surface/Supplier:
Item # 956914S - Silver Snowflake Bowl
Painters Paradise
111 Parrish Lane
Wilmington, Delaware 19810
(302) 478-7619 - Voice
(302) 478-9441 - Fax
jodecart@aol.com - email
<http://www.painterparadise.com>

Palette:
Deco Art Americana
Antique Maroon
Buttermilk
Gingerbread
Khaki Tan
Mauve
Mississippi Mud
Soft Black

Burnt Umber
Crimson Tide
Jade Green
Light Buttermilk
Midnight Green
Plantation Pine

Brushes:
Loew/Cornell Golden Taklon
Series 7550 Glaze/Wash No. 1/2
Series 7050 Script Liners No.18/0
Series 7000 Rounds No. 3
Series DM Stipplers No. 1/4, 1/8
Series Maxine Mops 1/2

INSTRUCTIONS

Step 1: No prep is needed, just basecoat the lid with Khaki Tan and then add a wash around the edge of the lid with Plantation Pine.

Step 2: Apply the pattern and basecoat as follows.

INITIAL BASECOATS

Snowman Face: Buttermilk
Holly: Jade Green
Berries: Mauve

SHADING AND DETAIL

❋ Float around the face/leaves/berries with Mississippi Mud; deepen in darkest areas with Burnt Umber. Float around the perimeter of the lid with Mississippi Mud and drybrush in the open areas (staying out of the shadows) with Buttermilk.

Snowman Face:

Step 1: Apply the pattern for the features; base the eyes and the mouth dots in Soft Black, and the nose in Gingerbread. After you shade and highlight, add the lashes and brows with Soft Black and the fine liner.

Step 2: Softly shade the face with Mississippi Mud under the leaves, the berries and to the left of the nose, eyes and mouth dots. Highlight with Light Buttermilk, walking the color out above the nose (where it is attached to his face) and on the top Right side of the head.

Step 3: Softly drybrush Crimson Tide onto his cheeks, using the DM Stippler. Add highlights in the eyes, mouth dots and cheeks with Light Buttermilk (fine liner). The nose is floated on both sides (small side-load) with Antique Maroon. Add lines with Burnt Umber through and under the nose. Highlight the nose with fine lines of Buttermilk across the top/center.

Leaves:

❋ Add the pattern for the center vein line if needed.

Step 1: With a side-load of Plantation Pine, float around all edges of the leaves, separate and define the leaves and with a broken float down the center vein line. *By broken float...I mean to lift the brush over where the separations (highlights) are/will be re-enforced. Deepen in the darkest areas with Midnight Green, such as where one leaf falls over another...or toward the base of the leaf, and if desired, enhance the dark edges of the leaves.

Step 2: Highlight first by dry brushing with Buttermilk in the wider areas of the leaf, using the small DM stippler and avoiding your shading areas. Using the fine liner, load into Jade plus a touch of Buttermilk, and pull a washy line down the center, and into a few of the separation marks. For the brightest highlight, load the liner in Buttermilk and tap it onto where the leaf would be the 'highest' or rounding out.

Step 3: With a soft side-load of Antique Maroon, float a glaze effect on the leaves. This is placed in one or two places on the leaf, you are not trying to change the color underneath...just enhance it a bit.

Berries:

Step 1: Shade the berries with Antique Maroon on the lower Left side and where they are hidden behind one another.

Step 2: Highlight with brush mix of Mauve and Buttermilk, on the upper Right side and lightly where they are falling in front of another. Add a highlight dash on the upper Right side, with Light Buttermilk.

Vines:

Step 1: The vines are stroked on with the fine liner loaded in Burnt Umber, and pulled through Buttermilk as needed to highlight. *If your colors become a bit muddy from stroking into one another, that is fine... I don't worry about that at all.

FINISHING DETAILS

Step 1: Erase any remaining graphite and spatter over the entire piece with Light Buttermilk.

Step 2: Varnish as desired. Enjoy!

~ xtra pattern ~

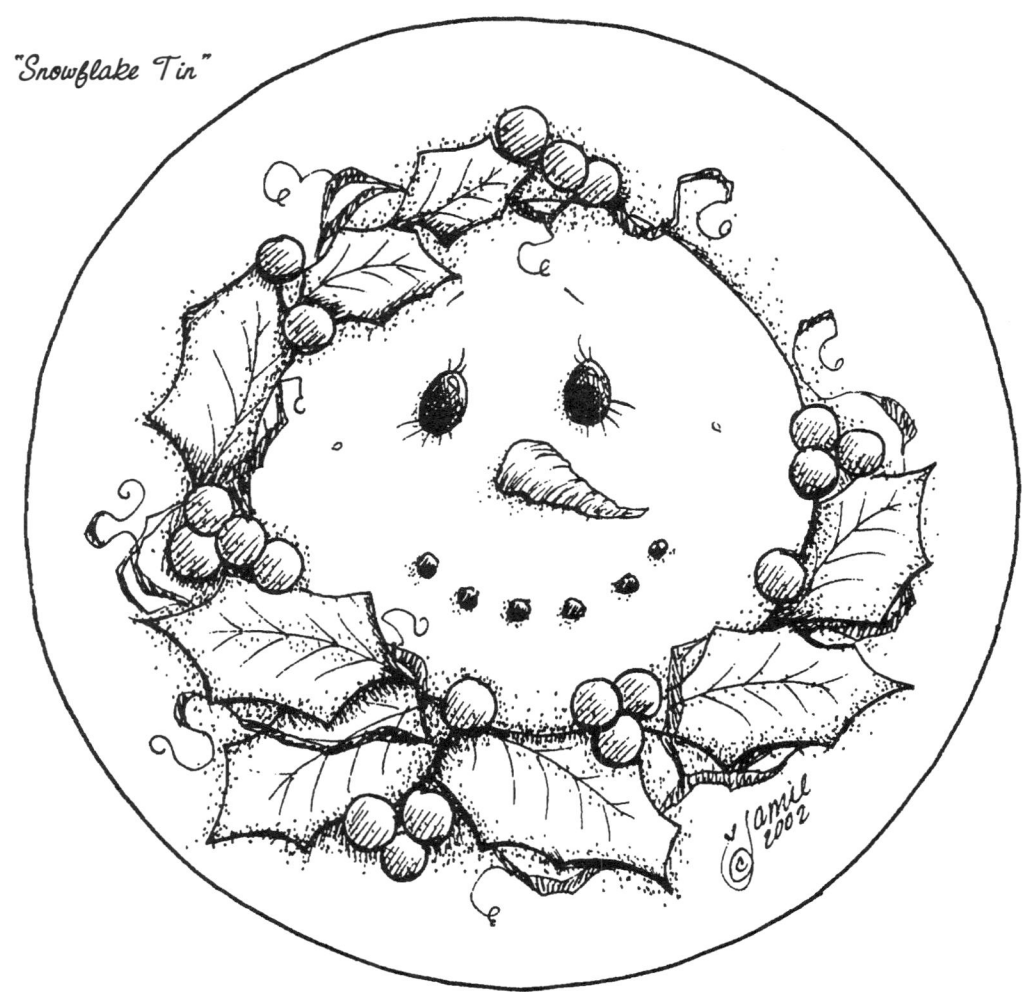

"Snowflake Tin"

"Trio of Wood Pots" - twig hearts

(Wood Pots) (color photo - inside back cover)

"The reverse side of these pots were painted with Snowman faces, but as an option...you could paint the twig hearts on all 'sides' of the pots, (I think 4 would look nice). Have fun!"

Surface/Supplier:
Trio of Pots w/Shelf
Be Creative
174 Oakdale Rd.
North York, Ontario
Canada   M3N 2S5
(416) 742-8535 or (416) 742-5575
(416) 742-1842 -Fax

Palette:

Deco Art Americana
Burnt Umber   Buttermilk
Deep Midnight Blue   Evergreen
Khaki Tan   Light Buttermilk
Mississippi Mud   Rookwood Red

Brushes:

Loew/Cornell Golden Taklon
Series 7550 Glaze/Wash No. 3/4, 1/2
Series 7300 Shaders No. 8, 2
Series 7050 Script Liners No. 18/0
Series Maxine's Mops No. 1/2

INSTRUCTIONS

Step 1: Sand, seal and sand again. *I left the inside raw wood, opting not to paint it.*

Step 2: Base the pots Buttermilk, the lids/bases in: Rookwood Red, Deep Midnight Blue and Evergreen. The shelf is based in Khaki Tan.

SHADING AND DETAIL

Twig Hearts:

Step 1: Apply the pattern for the heart; add checks with # 8 flat (and add a stylus dot) inside with the coordinating color:

Rookwood Red lid - check with wash of Rookwood Red

Deep Midnight Blue lid - check with wash of Deep Midnight Blue

Evergreen lid - check with a wash of Evergreen

Step 2: Shade along the bottom with Mississippi Mud and deepen with Burnt Umber. Highlight the tops with Light Buttermilk.

Step 3: Start forming the twig wreath with inky Burnt Umber, using the 18/0 liner.

Step 4: When you reach the desired thickness for your wreath, float around the heart-over the twigs- with Burnt Umber.

Vines and Leaves:

Step 1: The vines were stroked on with Burnt Umber, using the 18/0 liner. Shade here and there along the vines with Burnt Umber.

Step 2: The leaves were stroked on with Evergreen and the #2 flat.

Shelf:

Step 1: Shade and woodgrain with Mississippi Mud, highlight with Buttermilk. Deepen some of the woodgrain if desired, with Burnt Umber.

FINISHING DETAILS

Step 1: Erase any remaining graphite and varnish as desired.

"Trio of Wood Pots" twig pattern

"Trio of Wood Pots" - snowmen

(Wood Pots) (color photo - inside back cover)

"I just loved these little wooden pots when I first saw them...on the reverse side I painted twig hearts, so that you can turn them around during the remainder of the year. Have fun painting!"

Surface/Supplier:
Trio of Pots w/Shelf
Be Creative
174 Oakdale Rd.
North York, Ontario
Canada   M3N 2S5
(416) 742-8535 or (416) 742-5575
(416) 742-1842 -Fax

Palette:
Deco Art Americana

Burnt Sienna	Burnt Umber
Buttermilk	Deep Midnight Blue
Evergreen	Gingerbread
Khaki Tan	Mauve
Mississippi Mud	Rookwood Red
Soft Black	

Brushes:
Loew/Cornell Golden Taklon
Series 7550 Glaze/Wash No.
Series 7300 Shaders No. 2
Series 7150 Script Liners No. 18/0
Series Maxine's Mops No. 1/2
Series DM Stippler No. 3/8

(continued on page 54)

(continued from page 53)

INSTRUCTIONS

Step 1: Sand, seal and sand again. *I left the inside raw wood.

Step 2: Base the pots on Buttermilk, the hats/bases in Rookwood Red, Deep Midnight Blue and Evergreen. The shelf is based in Khaki Tan. Apply the pattern for the faces and basecoat as follows.

INITIAL BASECOATS

Mouth and Eyes: Soft Black

Noses: Gingerbread on the carrots, and a wash of Mauve on the other.

SHADING AND DETAIL

Faces:

Step 1: Shade with Mississippi Mud,

Step 2: The cheeks are drybrushed on with Rookwood Red, (DM Stippler) and the lips are floated with Rookwood Red. Add a highlight dot in the cheeks with Buttermilk.

Eyes:

Step 1: Highlight with Buttermilk.

Step 2: The lashes and brows are Soft Black.

Noses:

Step 1: Line and shade the carrot noses with Burnt Sienna.

Step 2: Shade with Rookwood Red; line the bottom with Soft Black.

Vines:

Step 1: With washy Burnt Umber and the 18/0 liner, stroke on the vines. Float around the vines here and there with Burnt Umber.

Step 2: The leaves are Evergreen, using the #2 flat.

FINISHING DETAILS

Step 1: Erase graphite and varnish as desired.

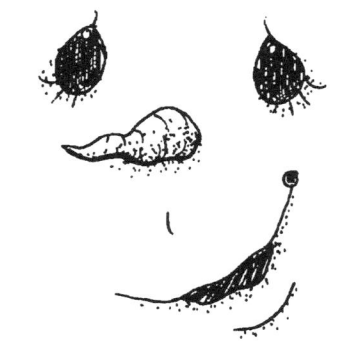

"Trio of Wood Pots" snowmen pattern

Jamie © 2002

"North Pole or Bust"

(Wood Basket) (color photo - inside back cover)

I used this box in "Between the Vines 5", and I had mentioned that I would paint another design for the flip side (if desired)...well, here is that design! Hope you enjoy!"

Surface/Supplier:
Wooden Basket w/Lid
Smooth Cut Wood
P.O. Box 507
Aurora, OR 97002
(503) 678-1318

Palette:
Deco Art Americana
Antique White
Burnt Orange
Buttermilk
Jade Green
Light Buttermilk
Mississippi Mud
Rookwood Red
Slate Grey
Uniform Blue
Burnt Umber
French Grey Blue
Khaki Tan
Mauve
Plantation Pine
Sable Brown
Soft Black

Brushes:
Loew/Cornell Golden Taklon
Series 7300 Shaders No. 4
Series 7550 Glaze/Wash Nos. 3/4, 1/2
Series 7050 Script Liner No. 18/0
Series DM Stippler No. 1/2, 1/4, 1/8
Series Maxine's Mops No. 3/4, 1/2

Misc. Supplies:
American Traditional "Snowflake" stencil (opt.)
Minwax "Early American" Stain/sealer
Deco Art Snow Tex (opt.)

INSTRUCTIONS
Step 1: Sand the lid, seal and sand again. Base the lid in Khaki Tan, the basket is stained with the Minwax "Early American" Stain/sealer or your favorite stain color.

Step 2: Apply the pattern and base-coat as follows.

INITIAL BASECOATS
Snowflakes: Softly stencil the snowflakes here and there on the lid, with Buttermilk. *Tip: I use a dry DM stippler and load it in the paint, tap most of it out on a paper towel, and then softly tap into the holes of the stencil.

Bag: Base in Antique White and then apply the pattern for the heart and base it in Buttermilk.

Mouse: Slate Grey; Ears are based in a mixture of 1/2 Mauve and 1/2 Buttermilk; Scarf is Mauve.

Snowman: Buttermilk; Scarf is based in French Grey Blue

Reindeer: Sable Brown; Ears/Antlers are Antique White; Scarf is Jade Green

SHADING AND DETAIL
Mouse:

Step 1: Shade with a brush mix of Soft Black and Slate Grey. Highlight with Light Buttermilk.

Step 2: Shade in the ears with Rookwood Red and highlight with Light Buttermilk. The hair on the head is Light Buttermilk. The stitches are Light Buttermilk.

Step 3: The features are Soft Black; the nose is Mauve, shaded on the bottom with Rookwood Red. Drybrush cheeks with Rookwood Red. The whiskers and highlights in the eyes, nose and cheeks are Light Buttermilk.

Step 4: The scarf is striped and shaded with Rookwood Red, highlighted with Light Buttermilk. The fringe is Rookwood Red.

Snowman:

Step 1: Shade with Mississippi Mud and highlight with Light Buttermilk.

Step 2: The features are Soft Black and the nose is Burnt Orange. The hair is stroked on with Light Buttermilk. The cheeks are drybrushed on with Rookwood Red. Highlights in the eyes and cheeks are Light Buttermilk. The buttons are Soft Black, highlight with Light Buttermilk.

Step 3: The scarf is striped and highlighted with Light Buttermilk. Shade with Uniform Blue. The fringe is Uniform Blue.

(continued on page 56)

(continued from page 55)

Reindeer:

Step 1: Shade with Burnt Umber and highlight with Antique White. Shade the ears with Rookwood Red; shade the antlers with Sable Brown and highlight with Light Buttermilk. The hair is Soft Black tipped in Buttermilk.

Step 2: The nose is Rookwood Red; the cheeks are drybrushed on with Rookwood Red. The features are Soft Black, highlights are Light Buttermilk. Stitch with Buttermilk.

Step 3: The scarf is dotted and shaded with Plantation Pine; highlight with Buttermilk. The fringe is Plantation Pine.

Bag:

* Shade and highlight the bag first, and then apply the pattern for the houses and paint them.

Step 1: Float the background, around the bag and animals, with Mississippi Mud. Deepen in the darkest areas with Burnt Umber, and then with Soft Black. Drybrush in the open areas with Buttermilk, float with Mississippi Mud on the edges of the lid. Check the outer edge with Plantation Pine.

Step 2: Shade the bag first with Mississippi Mud (on all edges/sides) except for the top rim. Deepen

"North Pole or Bust"

under the heart and pleats with Burnt Umber. Lastly float under the heart and in a few of the pleats with a touch of Soft Black.

Step 3: Drybrush in the open areas of the bag with Buttermilk, and float along the top rim with Buttermilk.

Step 4: Apply the pattern for the houses (we will float the color for the houses; not base-coat them in). All of the houses have Soft Black rooftops and holes...float Rookwood Red under the roofs of the red houses; float Plantation Pine under the roofs of the green houses; float Uniform Blue under the roofs of the blue houses. Highlight Buttermilk along the bottoms of the houses, and add a dash of Buttermilk in the holes. Float Mississippi Mud under the bottoms of each house, so that they stand out or separate from the bag.

Heart:

Step 1: Float the bottom of the heart with Mississippi Mud and highlight the top with Light Buttermilk. Check along the edge with Mississippi Mud and the #4 flat. The lettering is Burnt Umber using the 18/0 liner. The strings are Burnt Umber.

Snow:

Step 1: Float the snow on with layers of soft sideloads, using the following colors in order: Antique White, Buttermilk and then lastly with Light Buttermilk.

FINISHING DETAILS

Step 1: Spatter with Light Buttermilk, and add Snow Tex (opt.) on a few of the higher mounds.

Step 2: Erase any remaining graphite and varnish as desired. Happy Painting!

"Snow Sweet Snow"

(Wooden Canister) (color photo - back cover)

"Another unique piece from "Be Creative"! I think it would be neat to be able to leave this canister out all year round, so by painting something non-seasonal on the reverse side...such as a birdhouse, you could then turn it around and be able to use it through the year! Enjoy!"

Surface/Supplier:
Wooden Canister
Be Creative
174 Oakdale Rd.
North York, Ontario
Canada   M3N 2S5
(416) 742-8535 or (416) 742-5575
(416) 742-1842 -Fax

Palette:
Deco Art Americana
Burnt Orange
Buttermilk
French Grey Blue
Burnt Umber
Deep Midnight Blue
Jade Green
Light Buttermilk
Mississippi Mud
Plantation Pine
Soft Black
Deco Art Snow Tex (optional)
Mauve
Payne's Grey
Rookwood Red

Brushes:
Loew/Cornell Golden Taklon
Series 7550 Glaze/Wash No. 3/4, 1/2
Series 7300 Shaders Nos. 6, 1
Series 7050 Script Liners No. 13/0
Series 7000 Rounds No. 3
Series DM Stipplers No. 3/8,
Series Maxine Mops Nos. 3/4, 1/2

INSTRUCTIONS

Step 1: Sand, seal and sand again. Base the container in Deep Midnight Blue, the lid and knob in Buttermilk.

Step 2: Apply the pattern for the snowmen and basecoat as follows:

(continued on page 58)

(continued from page 57)

INITIAL BASECOATS

Snowmen/Jackets: Buttermilk

Hats (L-R):

Green hat: *Jade Green;*

Blue hat: *French Grey Blue w/ Mississippi Mud brim;*

Mauve hat: *Mauve (except the stippled area on the brim and pom-pom, which is left the background color).*

❄ Apply the pattern for the jackets, and to separate the snowmen. Float behind (next to) the snowmen with French Grey Blue...walking out the color to cast a glow over the scene.

SHADING AND DETAIL

All Snowmen:

Step 1: Shade the snowmen with Mississippi Mud, (make sure you float this color through where the jackets are, i.e.: The left snowman's right shoulder, where it is behind the small snowman). Refer to the line drawing for specific shading placement, (inked dots). Highlight with Light Buttermilk, on the faces, bellies, and hands, and by slip-slapping through the open areas of their lower bodies (staying out of the shadows).

Step 2: Float down the Right side of the snowmen's bodies with Payne's Grey...this should be very, very soft, so walk the color out on your palette before floating.

Step 3: The features are Soft Black, the carrot noses are Burnt Orange, and the round nose is a wash of Rookwood Red. Line underneath all noses with Burnt Umber. The carrot noses have detail lines and shading using Burnt Umber. The cheeks are all drybrushed on with Rookwood Red. Highlight the eyes, cheeks and noses with Light Buttermilk.

Step 4: The 'coal' buttons are all Soft Black, highlighted with Light Buttermilk.

Step 5: (The twig hair is painted after completing the hats.) Load the fine liner in Mississippi Mud and stroke through Burnt Umber and/or Buttermilk, as needed to define.

Jackets:
❄ Stripe all jackets with the #1 flat.

Green Jacket: *Stripe and shade with Plantation Pine. Outline and add ties with Plantation Pine. The little buttons are dots of Soft Black. Drybrush in the open area with Light Buttermilk.*

Blue Jacket: *Stripe with French Grey Blue and shade with French Grey Blue and deepen with Deep Midnight Blue. Outline and add ties with Deep Midnight Blue. The little buttons are Soft Black. Drybrush the highlights in the open areas with Light Buttermilk.*

Mauve Jacket: *Stripe and shade with Rookwood Red. Outline and add ties with Rookwood Red. The little buttons are Soft Black. Drybrush the highlight in the open areas, with Light Buttermilk.*

Hats:

Green Hat:

Step 1: Add large stripes with the #6 flat and Deep Midnight Blue, and over these stripes add a Light Buttermilk stripe. Between the blue stripes, line with Plantation Pine. Shade with Plantation Pine, and highlight with Light Buttermilk. The pom-pom is Jade Green...float Plantation Pine at the base of the pom-pom.

Blue Hat:

Step 1: Stripe with Deep Midnight Blue and Light Buttermilk; shade with Deep Midnight Blue and highlight with Light Buttermilk. The brim is shaded with Burnt Umber; highlighted and accent lined with Buttermilk. The button on top is Mississippi Mud, highlighted with Buttermilk.

Mauve Hat:

Step 1: Stripe the hat with Light Buttermilk, shade with Rookwood Red and highlight with Light Buttermilk. The brim and pom-pom are stippled on with the small stippler double-loaded with Mauve and Light Buttermilk. Tap blend on your palette, before moving to your project...re-load the brush and re-stipple as desired.

Greenery/Heart Wreaths:

Step 1: The heart wreaths are stippled on with the

1/4" DM stippler, double loaded in Plantation Pine and Jade Green, and then side-load the Jade Green edge in Light Buttermilk. Tap blend on your palette before moving to your surface. You may need to re-load your brush and re-stipple until you reach the desired opaqueness for your wreath.

Step 2: Add little 'roses' in your wreath with the #3 round, loaded in Rookwood Red and tipped into Light Buttermilk. Tap 3-4 times around in a circle to create the effect of the 'rose'.

Step 3: Add little leaves with the #1 flat loaded in Plantation Pine.

Step 4: The green 'rope' that is running through the wreaths is Plantation Pine tipped into Jade Green. Over-stroke the rope in a scalloped manner, using nearly straight paint (not a lot of water), and Plantation Pine.

Step 5: Float Plantation Pine on the snowmen, inside the heart. Shade under the heart with soft floats of Mississippi Mud.

Step 6: The wreath on the top of the lid is stippled on in the same manner as the heart wreaths, except that you will use the 3/8" DM Stippler. The 'roses' are stroked on with the #3 round (using more pressure will create a larger petal), same colors as in the heart wreaths. The leaves are stroked on with Plantation Pine, using the #6 flat. Float around the wreath with Plantation Pine, and in a few places with Mississippi Mud.

Snow:
Step 1: Float, (using the large flat and large mop), with Buttermilk first, and then with Light Buttermilk. Build up your floats gradually, until you reach the desired opaqueness.

FINISHING DETAILS

Step 1: Spatter over the scene with Light Buttermilk. Add Snow Tex if desired onto the top of the highest snow peaks.

Step 2: Check the lid with Mississippi Mud (1/2" flat). Shade with Mississippi Mud on the top and bottom of the lid. Dot Deep Midnight Blue dots in some of the checks.

Step 3: Erase any remaining graphite and varnish as desired. Enjoy!

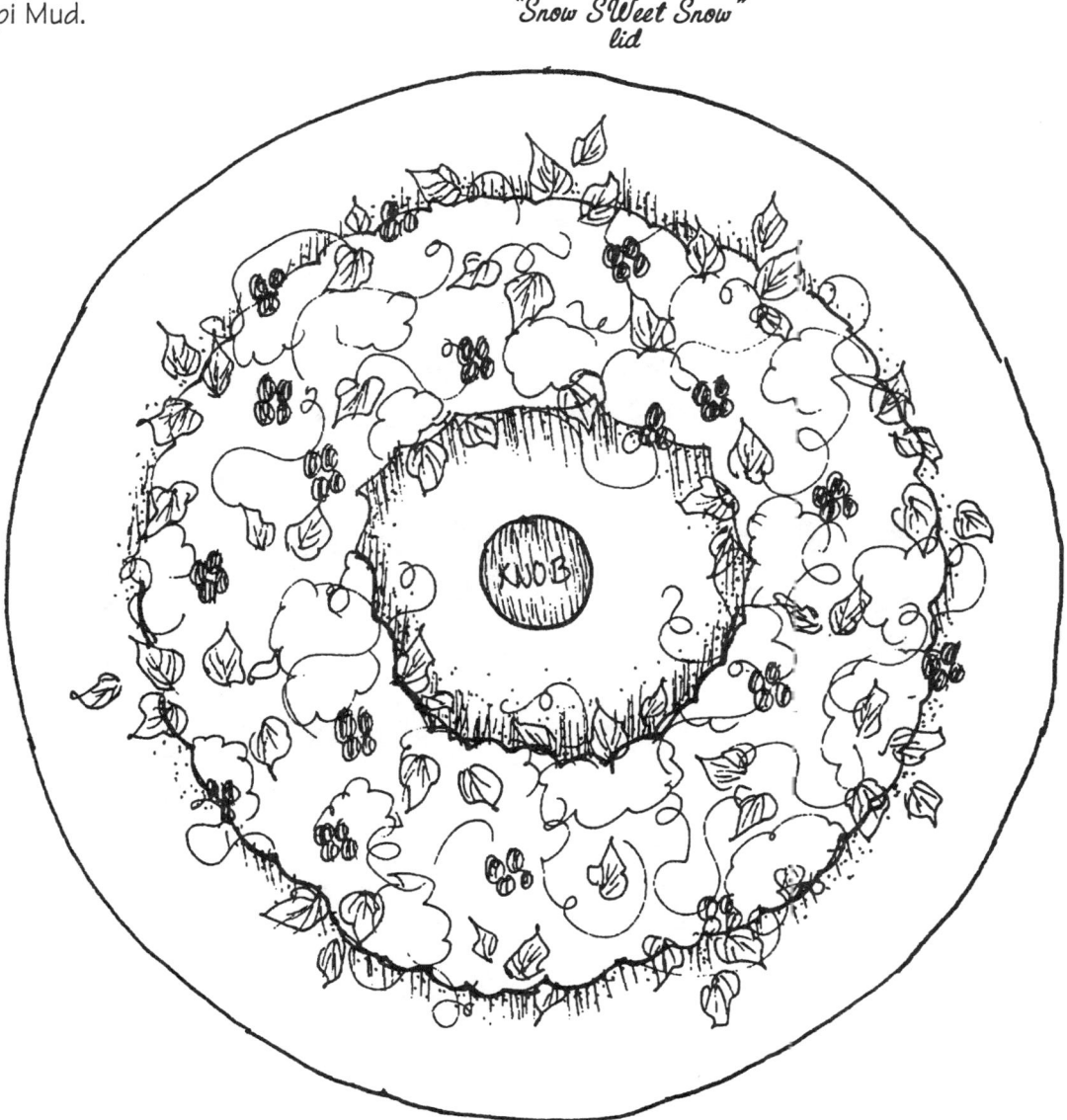

"Snow SWeet Snow" lid

"Snow Sweet Snow"

"Ring of Holly"

(Bowl) (color photo - back cover)

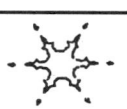

"A quick, fun little project to complete for gifts or for the holiday bazaars. I can see using this small, slightly oval bowl for candy or treats during the holidays. As an option, you can change the background color...maybe using Evergreen, Rookwood Red or Khaki Tan."

Surface/Supplier:
Hardwood Bowl - 6"dia. (slightly oval)
Viking Woodcrafts, Inc.
1317 8th St. SE
Waseca, MN 56093
(800) 328-0116 -Phone
(507) 835-3895 -Fax
viking@vikingwoodcrafts.com
http://www.vikingwoodcrafts.com

Palette:
Deco Art Americana

Burnt Orange	Burnt Umber
Buttermilk	Deep Midnight Blue
Evergreen	French Grey Blue
Jade Green	Light Buttermilk
Mauve	Mississippi Mud
Payne's Grey	Rookwood Red
Soft Black	

Brushes:
Loew/Cornell Golden Taklon
Series 7550 Glaze/Wash No. 1/2
Series 7300 Shaders Nos. 6
Series 7050 Script Liners No. 18/0
Series 7000 Rounds No. 3
Series DM Stipplers No. 1/2, 1/4
Series Maxine Mops Nos. 1/2

INSTRUCTIONS
Step 1: Sand, seal and sand again.
Step 2: Basecoat the bowl in Deep Midnight Blue.
Step 3: Apply the pattern and base as follows:

INITIAL BASECOATS
Snowman: Buttermilk (Stipple on the basecoat with the 1/2" DM Stippler).
Holly: Jade Green
Berries: Mauve
❄ *Apply the pattern for the features and base:*
Eyes/Brows/Mouth: Soft Black
Nose: Burnt Orange (medium wash)

SHADING AND DETAIL
❄ *Note: Shade the bowl, around the face, with Payne's Grey.*

Snowman:
Step 1: Softly float down the Left side of the face, under the eyes, nose and mouth with Mississippi Mud. Highlight above the mouth line and the nose with Light Buttermilk.
Step 2: Float a very soft side-load glaze of Deep Midnight Blue along the top of the head.
Step 3: Dry-brush the cheeks with Rookwood Red, and float Rookwood Red or the lower lip.
Step 4: With Burnt Umber, the nose is lined and then floated along the bottom edge. Add a highlight dash of Buttermilk along the top. Highlight in the eyes and cheeks with Light Buttermilk.

Holly:
❄ *Apply the pattern for the leaves if desired, and refer to the line drawing (inked dots) for shading placement, if needed.*
Step 1: With Evergreen, float the outer edges and behind the center line.
Step 2: Highlight with Buttermilk...along the inside edge and on the center line.
Step 3: Add vein lines with Evergreen. Add Buttermilk strokes around the leaves and glaze here and there on the leaves with Rookwood Red.

Berries: (Again...refer to the line drawing for shading, using the inked dots, if needed.)
Step 1: The berries are floated along the outer edge

(continued on page 62)

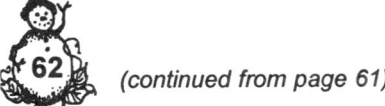

(continued from page 61)

with Rookwood Red, and highlighted along the inside edge with Buttermilk. Dot between the berries with Buttermilk.

Vines:

Step 1: The vines along the rim are inky Mississippi Mud, pulled through inky Burnt Umber and/or Buttermilk, as desired for brightness.

Checks:

Step 1: With the #6 flat loaded in French Grey Blue, stroke checks around the rim...pull them toward you. Add a dot between with Light Buttermilk. Shade just under them with Payne's Grey. Shade up on the brim on the inside edge with Payne's Grey and on the outside edge with French Grey Blue (soft floats- right over the vines).

FINISHING DETAILS

Step 1: Drybrush here and there on the bowl (around the berries and leaves) with Buttermilk, using the 1/4" DM Stippler.

Step 2: Erase any remaining graphite and varnish as desired. Happy Painting!

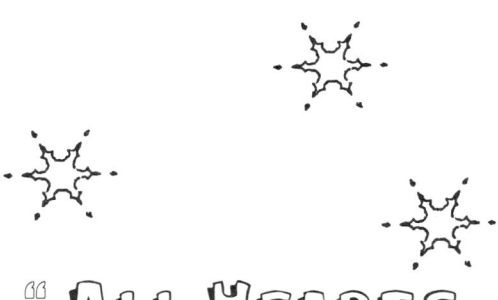

"All Hearts Come Home for Christmas"

"Ring of Holly"

CONTINUE...